What others are saying abou

"This is a ground breaking book that shows you how to develop unshakable levels of self-confidence in selling anything to anyone."

— Brian Tracy
Best-Selling Author of *The Psychology of Selling*

"As an avid learner of anything to do with influence it's commonplace to read books on 'how to close sales'. Then there's those who inform on getting the mind ready for the encounter with a customer, client or patient. Seldom though - is there anything that takes the whole persuasion process from 'soup to nuts' and lays it out in such a clear, concise structure as the one described in Leigh's brilliant book.

If you've a mind to be more persuasive. If you're certain 'sales' makes the commercial world go round. If you want to fully understand how ethical selling is the only way forward. Then you are in the right place - at the right time. Don't be too surprised just how persuasive this book is as it explains persuasion!"

— Peter Thomson
The UK's Most Prolific Information Product Creator

"One book can make all the difference! Books do change people's lives and over the years many have gone on to make me $100k - or more. This is one of those books you'll want to read over and over again, high-lite and also use as a tool. This is a book written by someone who understands selling, business and how to encourage the mind function at optimum. I can pretty much guarantee that when you come to the end of your career you will be able to look back at the books you read – and when it comes to working out those that made the difference to you, this will be one of them. Once I picked it up I couldn't put it down and I'm sure it will be the same for you. Enjoy!"

— Ron G Holland
Top Biz Guru and author of *The Eureka! Enigma*

"I love this book. It's just so different from the normal sales books around. Leigh tackles head on why some people smash their sales targets whilst others fall by the wayside – and shares her secrets on how anyone can improve their sales results.

In my view this book would be a valuable aid for anyone in selling – whether entering the sales sector for the first time or as a senior sales manager responsible for multi million pound sales targets. It's a unique exploration of how combining psychological techniques with conventional selling methods can produce sensational results."

— Penny Power
Co Founder of Ecademy and author of *Know Me, Like Me, Follow Me*

"In an ever changing and dynamic world, it is vital that we all learn the technique of sales – for we are all always selling, whether it be ourselves in a job interview, or a product or service for a business or a job. What leads people to fail is the lack of understanding of the sales process and the sales psyche, and this book proved just that understanding.

An easy to read, informative book about what really happens in your mind when you start to sell. The knowledge and ideas are presented with honesty and integrity and congruent with the building of long term and profitable sales generating relationships. It's an informative and practical guide to improving your sales – in any situation – and it has the added benefit that you will understand yourself better along the way. Read it!"

— Gill Fielding
Secret Millionaire and author of *The Book of Riches*

Unlock your winning sales mindset

Leigh Ashton

iSell – Unlock Your Winning Sales Mindset

First published in 2011 by Ecademy Press
48 St Vincent Drive, St Albans, Herts, AL1 5SJ
info@ecademy-press.com • www.ecademy-press.com

Printed and Bound by:
Lightning Source in the UK and USA

Cover and book design and typesetting by Ayd Instone

Printed on acid-free paper from managed forests. This book is printed on demand, so no copies will be remaindered or pulped.

ISBN-978-1-907722-66-0

A CIP catalogue record for this book is available from the British Library.

This book is dedicated to the Sales Professionals and Business Owners that strive to improve their minds in order to achieve greater things.

I hope the ideas in this book help you make changes that take you to the top of your game!

Thank You

My journey has been blessed with many words of wisdom and support from others. Without them I would most certainly be a very different person.

Thank you so very much...

My Mum and Dad
Jonathan Mills
Paul Ashton
Maria Millman
John Sproson
Martin Eldon
Daniel Priestley
Mindy Gibbins-Klein
Peter Thomson

...and to all the people that have touched my life and added to who I am of which there are so many!

To the greats that have inspired me...

Brian Tracy
Tony Robbins
Tad James

Contents

Introduction

Congratulations. Because you've picked up this book I can probably guess that you are either frustrated by the lack of sales results or that you just want more sales. Pat yourself on the back – you are in the minority that take action to do something about it. The question is will you read this book? Many people that buy a book of this kind don't get past the first chapter! Which one are you? How much do you want sales success?

I first came into the world of sales in 1984 and whilst it was a little scary for me as I'd switched from a career in banking...it was also very exciting. I soon realised that I loved this new world. Four years later when I was promoted to sales manager - and the frustration set in. Why did some people achieve their targets and some not? What was behind the varying behaviours and results that sales people had? Why couldn't they just do what I did to replicate the success that I had achieved? It seemed like common sense to me but either they didn't want to or couldn't...no matter how easy I thought it was.

This prompted a curiosity to learn more about the way people think and process. What I learned allowed me to change the way that people do and think about sales...and significantly increase their results in a way that was perfect for them. Not my way... their way.

The future world of sales

So much has changed since I got into sales.

OUT: Heavy handed pressure sales techniques, sales scripts, 'gift of the gab' sales winners, death by PowerPoint, 'all talking and no listening' pitches.

IN: Building genuine rapport, integrity and trust, long term win/win relationships and a positive consultative approach.

So if you're a member of the 'OUT' list – you need to change or you will likely become extinct.

Technology is changing fast, attitudes are changing, the selling arena is changing. There's social change...economic change...environmental change. Changes are changing!

You need to be one step ahead at all times if you're to achieve sales success.

There's a greater emphasis on psychology than ever before, both to understand yourself and your clients...and your future clients!

If you've ever had doubts or lacked the confidence or belief to achieve great sales results on a consistent basis...it's your own psychology that's getting in the way.

My outcome for this book is to:

- Help you identify your psychological barriers and give you some tools to overcome them
- Give you some insights on how your mind works so you can keep motivated and stay focussed
- Give you some pointers to identify the psychological patterns of your clients and prospects so that you connect with them at a deeper level and close more sales

Your goals for this book

It's really important to focus your mind on objectives when undertaking any activity. Reading this book needs to be useful to you...or there's no point in taking the time to read it unless there's value in it for you.

So what do you want to achieve from this book? What would need to happen for you to think that your time was very well spent?

Write down three important things you want to get from reading this book:

1. ....

   ....

2. ....

   ....

3. ....

   ....

This book is my way of sharing what I've learned, why it's useful, how you can use it to change your thinking and grow your sales success...no matter what level you're at...no matter what industry you're in.

So if you're ready...let's get started!

Leigh Ashton
London, 2011

1

How Your Thinking Determines Your Sales Success

"The mind is its own place and in itself, can make a Heaven of Hell, a Hell of Heaven."

— John Milton, Poet

Your amazing mind

Your mind has amazing potential. More than you can possibly imagine. It controls everything you do...most of which is completely unconscious. In fact about 95% of what you do is unconscious. You have no real awareness that it's going on...like the blinking of your eyes, breathing in and out, the blood running through your body, the pulse in your neck, your fingertips on this book and so much more. Until I mentioned them you gave those things no thought at all. They just happen.

Now that's fine when they have no consequence but sometimes they have very negative effects that get in the way of your success and that's what you will be exploring in this section. So if you have patterns of behaviour or thinking that get in your way, start to get excited because you are about to uncover these hidden and not so hidden gremlins and find out how to rid yourself of them for good.

Too good to be true? Keep reading with an open mind and make your judgement later. This has worked time and time again for thousands of people and it will work for you too.

So here's some theory for you. Your mind is split into two parts – the conscious and unconscious mind. Your conscious mind is the logical rational part of you that often talks you out of things. You unconscious mind is where the deep stuff is. It runs and protects your body. It stores your inner thoughts, values, beliefs and processes them to create the behaviours that serve you. In fact it really wants to serve you...so much so that it agrees with everything you tell it.

You unconscious doesn't know the difference between reality and fantasy so whatever you feed it...it will grow. It doesn't distinguish between good seeds or bad seeds. So what seeds are you planting? What you really need to know is that the unconscious mind drives you. Plant positive seeds and you'll reap the magic later. Sow negative seeds and you're destined to live your life in a sea of negativity.

For example...most people keep their car keys in the same place. You automatically go to that place without thinking. Then, one day you decide to store them somewhere that offers more security, so you move them from the shelf by the front door, to a cupboard in the next room. The first few times after you've moved your keys, you set off for the 'old' place. Over time, you retrain your unconscious mind to head towards the new location.

Leaving the car keys in the wrong place is relatively harmless stuff – but what about those mass of actions, thinking and habits that you have built up over the years. Many of these will serve you well. Yet other unconscious habits, actions and thoughts will undoubtedly be holding you back. And it's these negative unconscious habits that can be replaced with positive equivalents to catapult you to the success you desire.

Creating a great relationship with your unconscious mind is an essential part of creating success! Communicate with it on a regular basis. Get to know it. The more aware you are, the easier it is to get the sales success you want.

Communication is key

Having excellent communication skills is vital if you are going to achieve sales success.

When you communicate with others you are creating an experience for the other person. Everything you say has an impact...even the smallest things. What's interesting is that every word you use will have a unique interpretation for the person you are communicating with. When working with groups I often ask people the first thought that pops into their head when I say the word 'success'. Interestingly, no two people have ever come back with exactly the same response. Some say 'promotion', some say 'sitting on a beach', some say 'loving family', some say 'money'. And even if people say they thought of money...when questioned one may have seen a big house, the other the actual word came to mind or maybe a £ or $ image. So imagine a string of words in a sentence and a string of sentences in a conversation and you begin to realise how easy it is to create confusion or misunderstanding.

How does this happen? What causes the mind to do this? (Go with this, the figures coming up are astounding!)

You are subjected to over two million bits of information per second...and that's a conservative estimate. Your mind can only take in around 134 bits of information per second (that's 0.0067%). So imagine for a moment somebody giving you two million matches in your right hand and you take 134 of these matches into your left hand...every second. Now what do you think happens to the ones that are left in your right hand? They get discarded. What's more interesting is how you select the specific 134 each second. You will select the ones that are important or relevant to you and what's going on in your world right now. This is based on your beliefs, values and all your acquired life experiences and influences up to that point.

Focus of attention

If you believe the world is a rubbish place you will pick the information that supports your belief. Likewise if you believe the world is a great place full of opportunity then that's the information you will take. Remember your unconscious mind wants to support and agree with you. If you're having a bad day full of negative thoughts, it won't say 'Hey you, don't be such an idiot'. Remember that time you had a great meeting and closed the sale. You're great'. No – it just allows your negative thoughts to filter because that's the way you've trained it and it wants to please you.

The reason we all have different interpretations of the word 'success' is because our inner world is created from so many variations of the two million bits of information per second. We are all taking different 134 bit sections.

So what's the lesson here? Easy - What are you focussing on?

It's really important for you to continually focus on what you want rather than what you don't want. That way you create the thinking that allows you to take in the positive information that creates and supports your sales success. Doing anything else other than focussing on what you want will ultimately sabotage you – and your sales.

In life, you don't get what you want, you get what you expect so expect positive outcomes and you're more likely to get them. When you think that things are going to be tough that creates in you a behaviour that prepares you for that experience.

For example you're going to a meeting with a dissatisfied customer. All the way there you're thinking of all the things you're going to say in your defence. That puts you very firmly on the back foot and in your own space. Very likely you will enter that meeting with an air about you that could well instigate a heavy discussion. By visualising a positive outcome and putting yourself into their space, the behaviour you demonstrate will get a very different response.

Whatever your objective is when you communicate with prospective clients will impact on your expectation and if that's low or non-existent you may well find yourself creating the very lack of great results that you crave.

Think about it this way...put 'wealth' into Google and what do you get? Lots of websites to do with wealth! Put 'poverty' into Google and you get sites about poverty. Do they both exist? Of course they do. Focus on what you want, not what you don't want and you will notice it more and attract more of it.

I want you now to think about a problem you have in your area of sales generation. Once you have something specific in mind answer the following questions.

Go with your immediate response.

What is your problem?

....

....

Why is it a problem?

....

....

Why do you have this problem?

....

....

What caused it?

....

....

What are your limitations in solving it?

....

....

Who's to blame?

....

....

Why haven't you solved it yet?

....

....

Now do something else for at least 60 seconds that's completely unrelated before going onto the next part of the exercise.

Welcome back!

I now want you to think of the same issue and answer the following questions. Again, go with your immediate response.

What do you want?

....

....

How do you want it to be?

....

....

What do you need to get it?

....

....

What resources do you already have that will help you get this outcome?

....

....

Where are you with regards to achieving it?

....

What is the next step, which you can take towards getting your outcome?

....

When will you take this step?

....

So what did you notice?

The first set of questions would have focused you on the problem itself (what you don't want) and may have caused some negative emotions.

The second set of questions focused you on the solutions to your problem (what you want) and should have been more empowering. These questions also get your unconscious mind to come up with options for resolution.

Create positive self fulfilling prophecies by focusing on what you want and you will have already taken steps to greater sales success.

Different maps of the world

The map according to me, Leigh Ashton has been created from the moment I was born to this very day. All the people I've come into contact with, the experiences I've had, the reactions, significant emotional events...in fact everything that has occurred in my life. It's impossible for two people to have the exact same experiences in life and therefore impossible for people to have the same map of the world.

This is really important, so take note.

- When you communicate with anyone you absolutely must get into their map of the world to get deep levels of rapport.
- You need deep levels of rapport to uncover their true thinking. You need their true thinking to know if you can help them.
- You need to absolutely know that you can help them to create a mutually beneficial long lasting business relationship.

An indication that you are in the other person's map of the world is that you will be using *you* language. Every time you say 'we' you are in your map for example rather than 'we offer you....' it's more effective to say 'you will get....' Other than asking open questions you should be doing little of the talking.

Imagine for a moment going to a party. You see someone that looks interesting and start a conversation with a question. That person then goes on to talk and talk and talk about themselves the whole time. What's that like? Boring!!! Every time you meet with a prospective client and talk about your offering and the benefits you bring as a pitch at the start of the meeting...you become that boring person!

Find out about their map of the world, what's important to them, what problems they have and what they want to achieve...then and only then can you add value. Leave sales pitches to the sales talkers and become a listener and fixer.

Your perspective

There are so many ways of interpreting things that happen around us. Whatever your perspective in any given moment it is influenced by your map of the world. If you agree with me that everyone's map of the world is different, it's true to say that their interpretation is as real for them as yours is for you!

So who's right?

You both are! What's exciting about that is you can change your negative interpretation to a more positive perspective...if you can expand your thinking.

Think about a situation you have that's bothering you. What advice would you get from an alien, a pet, a great leader from history, a wise Indian chief or a comedian...in fact as many diverse characters as you can think of?

When you find yourself in an uncomfortable situation, always ask yourself...

What else could this mean?

You'll be able to come up with lots of alternatives to your current thinking and access many more choices to achieve your sales objectives.

It's been said that you don't know a person till you've walked a mile in their shoes. So take the time to reflect on what they may be thinking. Think about the possible ways they might interpret your actions or communication...incorrectly!! What possible alternative assumptions could they make? It's not always as simple or clear as you think.

The things that get in the way

The world isn't always kind to you. You'll get unexpected things hurled in your direction and the way you deal with these is crucial to your success. You have no control over other people or events that occur...but you do have total control over your reaction to them.

It's really important to understand what causes you to be unresourceful and get in the way of your sales success.

When you're not following through on stuff that you know would really make a difference to your sales success, ask yourself this really important question. *What stops me?* Find yourself a quiet place, grab yourself some paper and keep writing everything that comes into your head. When you get to a blank spot and think you've got it all...dig deeper and go beyond that.

When this happens a second time...dig even deeper. What comes beyond the second blank spot is normally the most helpful to you.

In my experience of working with sales professionals and business owners the barriers to success fall into two categories...regardless of the number of ways they manifest themselves.

First is the valley of reasons and excuses and the second is what you believe!

The valley of reasons and excuses

You may have already come across the concept of cause and effect. In simple forms it's how you react to people and situations outside of you.

It's far easier to blame the recession, cut's in budgets, lack of money, the boss won't let you or any other reason and excuse you can come up with. It lets you off the hook...it's not your fault!

Imagine you are in the land of delusion...which is about five miles west of the valley of reasons and excuses! The place where whatever you do, it's not going to have the effect you want because of someone or something else. These excuses become the mask you hide behind to explain your lack of results. Poor you. It's not your fault! You're such a victim.

These words may seem harsh to you and maybe they are but if you are to achieve great sales results you must put yourself at cause to be in control.

Staying in effect makes it impossible to give 100% to the actions that get results. Even when you believe you're trying hard...deep inside you'll be thinking it's all pointless because...

Putting yourself at cause is amazingly liberating...maybe a little scary but also exciting. More importantly it puts you in control. Being at cause doesn't mean ignoring the challenges, thinking positively and hoping they'll go away. It's about acknowledging the challenges and asking yourself 'so if all that is true...what action can I take to get me closer to where I want to be?' People at cause free their unconscious minds to come up with solutions to these constraints and become high achievers!

Take some time to focus on your own reasons and excuses.

What are the reasons and excuses you use most?

1 ....

2 ....

3 ....

4 ....

5 ....

6 ....

What impact do they have on your behaviour?

1 ....

2 ....

3 ....

4 ....

5 ....

6 ....

When you explore the reasons and excuses you use to make you feel better about your lack of sales success you can really start to move towards being at cause and taking action.

I was working with a sales team some years ago when one of the consultants said "I can't get my target because the company wants me to complete too much paperwork and it gets in the way". The word 'because' is a big clue that this is an 'effect' statement. I asked him... *'so if all that's true...what action can you take to get you closer to achieving target?'*. He then came up with 3 options that gave him more flexibility with his paperwork and allowed him to give more focus when with his clients and prospects. The following month he doubled his sales and smashed his target.

Your results are really up to you and what goes on in your head.

I have a belief that keeps me very firmly at 'cause' and that belief is *'I create everything that happens in my life by my actions and non actions'* So whatever happens in my life, I'm always asking myself 'what did I do to contribute to this happening?'

If you're not getting the sales results you want, I don't believe you have chosen to be in this situation consciously but I do think that where you are is the sum total of all the decisions you've made up to this point. Remember that your results are from activities carried out in the past...so at times when you allow yourself to be in 'effect' and take your foot off the accelerator...you will pay the price further down the line.

So when you hear yourself coming up with excuses, don't fall into the trap of believing them and ask yourself *'so if all that is true...what action can I take to get me closer to where I want to be?'*

What you believe

The second barrier that gets in the way of your success are the limiting beliefs you have. Some will be expressed openly like 'I'm not very good at networking', 'I can't talk to big groups' and 'I'm not a sales person'. Others will be hidden away deep down. So deep you don't even realise them yourself. That's the scary bit.

The *'what stops you'* writing exercise helps you uncover some of these and the next chapter will help show you how to get rid of them.

Find yourself a quiet space and give yourself plenty of time. Make sure you're not going to be disturbed. You'll need plenty of paper and a pen.

Now think about something that you avoid doing. Something that would really increase your sales success if only you just 'did it'

Write this at the top of the page and below it write *"What stops you?"*

Now it's down to you. Be completely honest with yourself and write everything that comes into your mind...even if it doesn't make sense.

Keep writing till you've finished then dig deeper and start writing again. You need to go beyond 2 of these blank spots before you're done. It's often what comes after the second blank spot that's the most useful.

In the next chapter you're going to find out exactly how you can overcome these barriers and achieve greater sales success.

Summary

This chapter has given you an insight into how you think, take in information, focus your attention, how you structure your map of the world and your inner barriers to sales success. You've explored your reasons and excuses and started to uncover your limiting beliefs. Phew!

Now what are you going to do with all you've learned in this chapter? How are you going to ensure you use it to create more sales?

It's all about action. Knowing and doing are two different things.

So what are your three priority actions that you're going to take as a result of reading this chapter?

1. ....

2. ....

3. ....

Now that you have some action points, put time in your diary to do them. Think about how you can make sure these happen...do you need an accountability buddy, do you need inspiring images around you to keep you on track or maybe it's something else for you. Whatever you need to make these happen...do it!

Also spend time thinking about the things that could get in the way of you completing these actions. What do you need to do to counteract these potential pitfalls? What's your contingency plan?

With that in place, go do them as quickly as you can...anytime **NOW** would be good.

2

How Your Beliefs Impact Your Thinking ...and Your Results

"If you believe you can or believe you can't ...you're right!"

— Henry Ford

How beliefs are created

From the moment you were born you were subjected to information, emotions and the influence of others. You will have reacted in your own way to these events and created beliefs around them. Some of your beliefs will be really positive and empowering...some of mine are...Mum and Dad are always here for me and love me. All living creatures deserve respect and kindness. I can be whoever or whatever I want to be.

What are your positive beliefs? You will know what some of yours are for you. These beliefs create a really solid foundation for us to build on for our entire lives. Go back to them often for reassurance, inspiration and motivation.

Your beliefs are core to who you are and you will always defend them no matter what. The most heated debates and arguments are caused by people defending their opposing beliefs. Whether they are based on reality or fantasy doesn't impact on the power of your beliefs. They are yours and therefore very real to you.

In addition to our positive and empowering beliefs, there are beliefs that affect us in a negative way. These are called limiting beliefs. They remind you of your fears and inadequacies. They stop you taking action.

Your limiting beliefs are already in place by the time you are 7 years old. From the moment you're born to age 7 years your mind is like a sponge soaking in everything that happens around you. These are the imprint years. Everything you take in during this time will be interpreted by your very young self.

At this age you have no life experiences to draw on...or adult intellect. It's hardly surprising then that you may have made an unhelpful interpretation that you then carry with you into adulthood.

Let's give you an example. You are helping an adult in your home or garden and really doing your best to do a great job. The adult says to you 'no, no, no...you don't do it like that. Give me that here. I'll do it.' Now this is all done with love and kindness in the hope of teaching you some kind of lesson. The next time you try really hard to get it right and the adult says to you 'no, no, no...you don't do it like that. Give me that here. I'll do it.' Now you're feeling that you may not be good at this stuff. So the next time you try even harder and you think you've done a great job when you hear... 'no, no, no...you don't do it like that. Give me that here. I'll do it.' Well now you know. You are just not good enough for this job and stop trying. You only need to hear something a handful of times before you start to believe that you can't do this stuff! When you're less than 7 years old you haven't got the intellect to work things out in your head so you decide on the easiest option...the one you understand...you're just not good enough!

Imagine this limiting belief goes unchallenged...even though you've achieved lots as an adult. It's lurking deep inside you...and springs into action every time you're doing something for the first time. It stops you learning new things or giving 100%. It's also a great fallback position when you fail to get the result you want. So you settle for less!

Now I don't know whether this belief has any resonance with you or not. It's just an example. If it did...celebrate because at least you know it's there...inside you.

You may or may not remember specific events that led to you creating your limiting beliefs but every day since you will have focused on reinforcing them with events that happen in your everyday life. Remember that you will only take in 134 bits of information per second so those times where you have exhibited the opposite behaviour...when you achieved exactly what you want in the way you want it...well you'll have just discarded those!

Some years ago I was working with a Sales Manager. She arrived before everyone in the morning and left after everyone in the evening. She raced around all day getting as much done as she could. Always striving to do more, lead and motivate her team more effectively, increase sales...the list goes on. She was exhausted and I quietly wondered how she was holding this together.

As a child of 4 she had an opportunity to start school early...she was a very bright child! Her parents took her to the school for a meeting with the teacher to discuss the options. During this meeting her parents and the teacher chatted about whether she was ready for school...was she good enough...or should they let her have an extra year of play. All this was done with love and kindness and her best interest at heart. The only words she focused on were 'was she good enough' and remembered very clearly the feelings of inadequacy she felt as a child. This had caused her to push herself to do more and more rather than achieving the desired outcome. Once she had the realisation that she was actually more than good enough she was able to let go of the limiting belief and focus on getting results. Being busy isn't necessarily being productive. Her hours at work reduced and her results went up!

Limiting beliefs fall into 3 categories:

Hopelessness – this is the belief that it's impossible for anyone to achieve a particular thing

Helplessness – this is the belief that others can achieve this but not you

Worthlessness – this is the belief that you are not good enough or don't deserve success

One limiting belief on its own has the power to stop you achieving the sales success you desire. It really doesn't matter how much sales training you have if you have a limiting belief that gets in the way of you consistently carrying out the behaviour they teach you.

If you're not achieving the success you want in sales, it's quite likely that limiting beliefs are at play. You may know some of them consciously. You may not! However, you definitely need to identify those that are unconscious too.

The great news is that you can change your beliefs. You will have already done this for yourself without even realising. When you were a small child, you may well have believed in Father Christmas or the tooth fairy. Do you believe in them today? Yeah I know...I just spoiled it for you ☺. Think about all the things you believed as a child that you no longer believe.

They used to believe the world was flat...and stone people to death if they put forward a new theory! Remember that you will defend your beliefs at all times...whether they support you or not.

It's also worth pointing out that all your limiting beliefs that affect your sales results will also be affecting other areas of your life. Start to notice patterns and become more aware of what your beliefs are.

Your beliefs around sales

So who do you think you are? What beliefs do you have about yourself? What beliefs do you have about others in the sales process?

You will have uncovered some of your limiting beliefs around sales in the previous exercise, so let's get a little more specific.

Take a look at the following statements and score them between 0–100%. 0 being you completely disagree and 100 being you completely agree.

	% True for you
You	
I am a great sales person	
I believe I can sell well	
I have the ability to sell	
I know how to sell	
I can only sell if I am in the right place at the right time	
Selling	
Is about assisting the customer to choose the most appropriate way of moving forward	
Is an honourable way to make money	
Is easy	
Customer	
The customer really wants to know about my offer	
The customer will be pleased to see/hear from me	
The customer will buy once they understand the benefits of the service/product on offer	

My Company

Offers great customer service

Offers a great return on investment

Deserves to be highly successful

Cares about you

Provides all the support you could wish for

No matter how many times I do this exercise within companies, the responses are always so varied within the same team. So what do your responses say about you? Your scores are all clues to what's going on below the surface. Your beliefs impact on your behaviour, so if you have a low score against 'I am a great sales person' how do you think that impacts on your sales? How much commitment do you have if you have a low score here? Even if you think you're committed it's very unlikely that your behaviour will consistently reflect this. Whatever is going on inside you will win...believe me!!

How you reinforce your limiting beliefs

When you have beliefs that limit you in some way, you will go out of your way to find evidence to support your belief. Say for example you score yourself low on 'the customer really wants to know about my offer'. Every time you have a conversation with a prospective customer that doesn't get a positive result, you deposit that experience in your Limiting Belief Fund. All the occasions where you had a fabulous result get discarded. You place no importance on them at all...just because they are not in alignment with your belief. It is sad and true!

One of my clients witnessed an incident as a child when her mother verbally abused a salesman that came to their house. Her memory of the experience was unpleasant and shaped her thoughts around sales. She came to me because she is an artist and found it impossible to promote herself or her art. Whilst she had been successful in the past...the sales element had always been brokered by an agent. By revisiting her beliefs around sales and selling she was able to overcome her limiting beliefs and create empowering thoughts and actions that helped her to promote her art and make great sales...and direct her agent more effectively. It's no wonder that she avoided sales. Her fear of the potential repercussions she may experience with buyers was causing her unconscious mind to keep her safe by avoiding sales altogether!

Another thing to consider is the positive impact of your belief. All behaviour has a positive intention and even though your belief limits you in some way, the pain of that limitation is not enough for you to take alternative action. Why is that? It's because you get some kind of payback...let me explain.

Have you ever planned to spend time on the telephone making new business development calls? You travel to work full of good intentions. You have thought about how many calls you were going to make and what approach you were going to use. You have visualised a positive outcome at the end of your telephone session. Then you get to work and make yourself a hot drink...maybe have some breakfast. You decide to check your emails in case any orders arrived overnight. You reply to some emails...then check your social networks...then have a conversation with a colleague about a project...then before you know it the morning has gone. Familiar?

If you have a limiting belief that prospective customers don't want to know about your offer and that you are being a nuisance by calling them out of the blue...then you have successfully avoided the potential rejection you might have to deal with. The other stuff is more comfortable for you. Even though you know this would make a massive difference to your sales you avoid it like the plague. Should you be forced into a position where you have no place to hide and you eventually pick up the phone to make these calls, you have so much angst internally that a positive outcome is unlikely.

Until you deal with these limiting beliefs it's going to be a challenge to get the sales results you want and practically impossible to enjoy the process.

Eliminating your limiting beliefs

How would you like a simple process that helps you get rid of your limiting beliefs? A process that's so simple you can use it again and again!

You will need to complete the writing exercise 'What Stops You' beforehand so if you haven't done it yet...stop reading and start writing! Here's a reminder if you haven't done it yet.

> Find yourself a quiet space and give yourself plenty of time. Make sure you're not going to be disturbed. You'll need plenty of paper and a pen.
>
> Now think about something that you avoid doing. Something that would really increase your sales success if only you just 'did it'
>
> Write this at the top of the page and below it write "What stops you?"

Now it's down to you. Be completely honest with yourself and write everything that comes into your mind...even if it doesn't make sense.

Keep writing till you've finished then dig deeper and start writing again. You need to go beyond 2 of these blank spots before you're done. It's often what comes after the second blank spot that's the most useful.

Go through what you have written and highlight every limiting belief. Pick the one that will have the greatest impact on your sales success once it's eliminated.

Are you ready to let go of this limiting belief with the *Belief Buster*?

ESSENTIAL - Only continue with this process if you get a committed 100% yes response!

Your Limiting Belief is:

....

....

....

....

The following questions will help you connect with the problems this limiting belief is creating for you and the potential consequences if you hold onto it. You'll also explore the positive outcomes of letting it go.

How has this Limiting Belief blocked you in the past? What has it stopped you doing/achieving?

....

....

....

....

....

What will you ultimately lose if you don't let go of it?

....

....

....

....

....

Why are you totally committed to letting it go?

....

....

....

....

....

The following questions will destabilise your limiting belief, create a void for you to fill with a more empowering belief and reinforce the positive results of your belief change.

Question the Belief

Why do you believe this?

....

....

....

....

When did you take on the belief? (Remember, beliefs often get formed before the age of seven and you may not be consciously aware of when).

....

....

....

....

What higher level belief may you have formed about yourself that would have caused you to take this belief on? Common higher level beliefs might be "I don't deserve", "It's wrong to ask/want things?"

....

....

....

How has this limiting belief served you in a positive way in the past? Where has it been useful?

....

....

....

....

Think of 3 Counter Examples

Where has this belief not been true for you?

....

....

....

Who might not believe this is true of you?

....

....

....

....

....

When was this not true for you?

....

....

....

....

....

When have you done something that contradicted this belief?

....

....

....

....

....

Think of a More Empowering Belief

Identify an empowering belief that would support you in achieving greater sales success.

Your new Empowering Belief is:

....

....

....

....

Where/when have you acted as if this were true?

....

....

....

....

What were the positive consequences for you?

....

....

....

....

Where could you practice/continue doing this?

....

....

....

....

Visualise yourself holding this empowering belief.

Pick three contexts where you would use this and run through each one.

....

....

....

What will you do differently now that you have changed?

....

....

....

....

How do you feel about that old belief now?

....

....

....

....

Can you even remember what it was?

You should be feeling pretty good now...awesome in fact. You can use the *Belief Buster* as many times as you need to...whenever you want to. The more limiting beliefs you deal with, the more sales success you will have.

It doesn't stop there...getting rid of your limiting beliefs will have a positive impact on all areas of your life so expect more success generally!

To Summarise

In this chapter you've really explored your beliefs...specifically those that get in the way of your sales success. You've used a process to elicit your limiting beliefs, eliminate them and replace them with a positive more empowering belief.

It's fair to say that if you've had difficulty letting go of a limiting belief you'll be holding onto it for deep rooted reasons...and may need the help of a coach. Please either contact me or find yourself a coach that can help you work it out.

What are your three priority actions that you're going to take as a result of reading this chapter?

1. ....
2. ....
3. ....

Go do them as quickly as you can

...anytime **NOW** would be good.

3 Sales and the Inner You

"Human beings...by changing the inner attitudes of their minds can change the outer aspects of their lives."

— William James Mayo

Friend or Foe

I believe that your inner voice is your unconscious mind and its primary function is to look after you and keep you safe. It's great when your inner voice is saying positive and empowering things to you. Take a moment to think of the things it says to you when you are doing something that you are really good at. It will reinforce your strengths and capabilities and make you feel amazing.

However what about when you do new stuff or stuff outside of your comfort zone? Or maybe when you've made a mistake or screwed up? This is when you're most likely to hear the other side of your unconscious mind...your inner critic!

Who is your inner critic? Who is the person you hear in your head when things don't go as planned?

Everything you hear has been created or chosen by you. It's all the stuff you've heard from others in your life mashed together with your inner fears. It's useful to remember that at some level this stuff has served you positively so let's not throw the baby out with the bath water just yet. Your inner voice is your best friend too...warning you of any looming danger. The real issue here is controlling your inner critic so that you get the positive benefit without the debilitating effects of negativity.

At about the age of 7 our unconscious mind splits from our conscious mind and it's at this point that you become fragmented in your thinking. It's possible to have values and beliefs that are in conflict with one another.

You might want to think about the voice you hear. Is it yours?

> I remember delivering a workshop when this very topic came up and a woman in the audience told us that she knew she was very capable to achieve what she wanted but every time she told herself she could, she heard a voice that said "Oh no you can't". I asked her whose voice it was and I could see that she was surprised by the response she got. "Oh my...it's my ex-husbands voice...and we've been divorced for 10 years"

So whose voice do you hear in your head?

Whether your inner voice is saying positive or negative things it's really important to recognise that there's a positive intention in the message. What could it be for you? Maybe you haven't had great success with a new sales strategy or technique and it causes you lots of angst every time you try it. Or there's a particular client or prospect that takes lots of your energy to communicate with. One positive intention is to stop you feeling the pain of the disappointment or the trauma of communicating with this person...so let's not bother doing it again...just in case there's some pain here. That would be great if it weren't such a useful tool to increase your sales or potential for future business. You may avoid the short term pain but the long term impact is that you won't get any better at your craft and your sales are less likely to increase. Sound familiar?

It's really useful to think about the positive intention when your inner critic stops you moving forward. Once you know what the positive intention is you can incorporate it in another way, which will allow you to focus on the task in hand and keep the inner critic happy at the same time!

Start recording the negative things your inner critic says and ask yourself the following questions:

Whose voice is this?

What is the positive intention of this message?

How can you preserve the positive intention in your new strategy?

These questions will give you a greater awareness of what's going on within you and give you greater control. They allow you to make friends with your unconscious mind and change your reaction to that inner voice. Rather than letting it crush you...you can be curious to the reasons behind it. Understanding what's going on behind the voice will ultimately give you more control to change the voice!

> Back to the lady with the ex-husband inner critic...she told me the voice was coming in through her left ear as if her husband was sitting on her shoulder. I asked her to move him to the corner of the room and she said his voice had become quieter. I asked her to put him in the corridor outside and his voice vanished. Now she has a strategy to remove him if she ever hears his voice again!

Ultimately it's your choice how you react...you have the control...so what are you going to choose?

The importance of language

The language you use internally has a huge impact on your behaviour. If you say things are hard...guess what, they are. If you say things are less than easy you get a very different internal response. Think about the words you use to yourself? Are you making things tougher than they need to be?

Many of my friends get concerned when they get a sore throat "I do hope I'm not getting a cold" they say. Dangerous talk, I think! Your brain doesn't actually process negatives. What happens when I say "don't think of a blue tree"...you think of a blue tree right! That's because you can't not think about something that you don't want to think about, without thinking about it first. So when you say "I do hope I'm not getting a cold", you are focusing your mind on the words "getting a cold" and manifesting the very climate for a cold to take hold. Deepak Chopra (M.D. and founder of the Chopra Center for Wellbeing) says "your immune system is constantly eavesdropping on your internal dialogue"...and it's not just your immune system!

Every time you don't want something to happen, your focus of attention is fixed right on it. I hope...this isn't going to be a tough sales meeting...they don't say no...the client isn't challenging – these are all versions of "don't think of a blue tree!"

Now let's get real here...I don't deny that the world sets us certain obstacles to overcome but I do believe that the obstacles are easier to overcome when we use positive language!

Rather than saying "This is really hard" you could say, "this may not be easy right now but it will get easier each time I practice". Positive words create a very different internal state that is much more empowering and resourceful...and with that comes more success.

> You may be interested in my strategy for when I get a sore throat. Firstly, I thank my unconscious mind for alerting me to the fact I need to take it easy and promise to get an early night. I then instruct my immune system to do its stuff while I'm asleep and make me feel amazing the next morning.
>
> Works every time.

Even the most positive sales people can fall into the trap of negative language so start to notice when you do this yourself.

Every time you hear yourself use negative language reframe the comment using positive language that's framed on what you want rather than what you don't want.

Chunking Up

Another area of language that will really help you is the concept of chunking. Do you focus on the small detail or are you a big picture thinker?

Your mind finds it easier to focus on between 5 – 9 chunks of information at any one time...so the more detailed your thinking the more likely you are to go into a state of overwhelm. *Focus on the outcome you want and stay in the big picture.*

An easy way to do this is to focus on the area in which you are overwhelmed and ask yourself the following questions:

For what purpose are you doing this?

....

....

What will this do for you?

....

....

....

What is important about this?

....

....

What is your positive intention?

....

....

These questions will always take you to higher levels of thinking and can often resolve your issues on their own.

The sum of the parts

You may sometimes find that you are in conflict with yourself. Part of you wants to make those sales calls and part of you would rather do your sales admin.

These conflicts will have a serious impact on your sales because you will generally take the easy option. By examining the parts that are in conflict you can often resolve the issue and get back on track.

> I was coaching a sales person some time ago who was procrastinating over picking up the phone to make business development calls. She knew that if she increased the volume of calls she would increase her sales. She told me that she was completely committed to increasing her sales but every time she arrived at work with the intention to get the calls done she allowed 'stuff' to get in the way and before she knew it, it was the end of the day and the calls still hadn't been made. Firstly we explored the positive intention for both parts. One part had a starting point of wanting to make new connections and the other feared rejection. By exploring the bigger picture she discovered that both sides had a higher intention of wanting sales success and ultimately happiness. Once her unconscious mind realised that at a higher level both parts wanted the same thing she was able to let go of the fear of rejection and got straight on the phone with real enthusiasm.

We used the following process to uncover the positive intentions of each part and finished the session by uniting the conflicting parts. Because you will be resolving your inner conflict at an unconscious level you'll require a little imagination for this next technique. Please read all the steps beforehand.

Step One, Identify the parts

Hold both of your hands in front of you so that your palms are facing the ceiling. Look at the first hand and imagine that you are holding the first part on it and try to imagine the shape of the part. Some people see it as a glowing ball, some see it as one of their parents and others see more weird things so just visualize the shape that feels right for you. Notice if the part has a weight or if there's any sound. Do the same for the second part. You're using symbols here because your unconscious mind works best using symbols.

Ask your first part about its positive intention: Look at the first part and ask it "what is your positive intention?" and keep asking "For what purpose?" until you have reached the highest intention. This will normally be one of your values like happiness or similar.

Ask your second part about its positive intention

Do the same with your second part until you have reached the highest intention. Your goal is to allow your two parts to agree on a common value like happiness or similar. The more you go up the hierarchy of positive intentions the more you'll find that the two parts both want the same thing.

Bring them together

Talk to both parts and tell them that they both have the same intention and that there's no need for a conflict. You should now notice that your hands are coming closer and closer together of their own accord...and eventually touch. Once your hands touch each other hold them together firmly and this will send a clear message to your unconscious mind that the conflict is now resolved.

This simple visualisation technique will really help you to overcome inner conflicts that get in the way of your sales success. Remember that when visualising, you get what you get so just go with it. Trust your unconscious mind to give you exactly what you need...it always does. Have fun with this process and it will allow you to resolve stuff that's been an issue for you...maybe for a long long time!

Don't be fooled into thinking that it's too simple to be truly effective. I've worked with sales people that have transformed their thinking...and their sales results with this process.

Have an open mind, a curiosity to explore and a focus on the positive outcome you want...and watch your sales go up!

To Summarise

In this chapter you've discovered how your inner dialogue impacts on your success, the power of using positive language, how chunking up helps you maintain control and how to overcome inner conflicts.

What are your three priority actions that you're going to take as a result of reading this chapter?

1. ....

2. ....

3. ....

Go do them as quickly as you can ...anytime **NOW** would be good.

4

Putting Yourself in the Right State of Mind

"Just as your car runs more smoothly and requires less energy to go faster and farther when the wheels are in perfect alignment, you perform better when your thoughts, feelings, emotions, goals, and values are in balance."

— Brian Tracy

How your state of mind impacts on your sales success

Everything you experience has an impact on you...it can't not. Some have a positive impact and some negative...and others somewhere in between. It's how you interpret the experience that makes the difference!

The information you're taking in goes through your internal process and you come up with an internal representation of what it means to you. Once you've decided on what that is, you will react in accordance with your internal representation.

Think about it this way...you make a call to a prospect that you think is going to buy and they tell you they have decided to buy from a competitor. You're really disappointed and do all you can to explore their decision in the hope that you can change their thinking. The prospect sticks with their decision – end of conversation.

How you process that internally is now up to you. Do you think it's all so unfair? Does it ruin your whole day? Are you so emotionally upset that you stop putting in any real effort to making other sales happen?

Well that's one response!

Alternatively...straight after the call you decide what changes you're going to make to your approach to limit the risk of this happening again. You explore every step of your strategy and learn from it. You reflect on the buying strategy of the prospect so that when you talk with them again you know exactly how they buy...and tweak your approach to suit them!

How much more in control will you be if you use this approach instead?

If you're thinking "Yeah, right...it's not that easy"....you're in serious trouble. With thinking like that you'll never make the choices that keep you in control.

You can start small with things that have a limited negative impact on you. Practice the alternative way of thinking and see what happens. Once you've mastered this with little things you'll strengthen your ability to do this with more challenging experiences.

Imagine...reacting in a completely controlled and positive way...how many more sales do you think you'll achieve? Only you know the answer to that but what I can tell you is that when I coach people in this area and they incorporate this approach, it transforms their results. It's impossible for this thinking not to have a positive impact when practised.

By the way...it's not only in sales where you can use this! You will attain more success in all areas of your life if you think like this.

Good state...Bad state

Now there are some things you can do to make managing your state even easier. You already have stuff that puts you in a positive state. It could be photo's of loved ones, pictures of beautiful places you want to visit...or stuff you'll buy with your commission, it may be a piece of music or a speech that inspires you, or it may be your cuddly teddy bear! I don't know what these things are for you but you do.

Make a list now of all the things you already know put you in a positive state of mind.

Be sure to write things that you have control over. I know sunshine works for many people but there's not too much chance of sunshine in the winter months so you need things that help you at any time...regardless of what's going on in the world!

Things that put you in a positive state

1. ....
2. ....
3. ....
4. ....
5. ....
6. ....

Whatever these things are for you, have them close at hand so you have access to them whenever you sense your state dropping. It makes more sense to take a few minutes reinforcing your positive state than to soldier on when you're not feeling great inside.

There are also some physical things you can do when you're feeling unresourceful. A great tip is to stand up and look upwards...smiling. It's impossible to feel down when you do this. Go on try it now. Stand up; look at the ceiling with the biggest smile you can manage. Now without moving a muscle, pretend to be depressed! Told you...it always works. You may get some odd looks but who cares when you feel this good.

Never underestimate the power on these techniques and props. One of the sales people I was working with had a huge insight when I covered this topic in a training session. He always arrived positive and ready for action. Except on a Monday. Monday was different. It took him ages to get into a good state and he just put it down to the fact it was Monday...you may relate to this ☺ What he realised during this exercise is that he travelled to work listening to upbeat music on his iPod. It really set him up for the day. On Friday he went out for a beer with his work colleagues and left his iPod at the office. Being without his iPod on Monday morning had taken his motivating and uplifting music out of his routine! He solved the problem by buying another iPod so he always had access to his music.

It's also worth exploring the triggers that put you in a negative state. You will be aware of some of them but there will be others that you won't have a conscious awareness of. These are the triggers that switch your state without you even noticing. Start a diary of when you find yourself in a negative state of mind. What happened immediately beforehand that caused the change?

Having a greater understanding of these triggers gives you more control and you'll be able to maintain your state even more just by knowing them.

Start off listing the triggers you already know:

1. ....

2. ....

3. ....

4. ....

5. ....

6. ....

There are only two things you can change when dealing with your triggers...either your attitude or your behaviour!

If you're in a situation that is causing a negative reaction in you, answer the following questions:

What's another meaning you can give to this?

....

....

How can you change your behaviour to get a different response?

....

....

How does this change your internal reaction to each one?

....

....

Remember to incorporate positive language in your thinking and your impact on others.

Another area well worth exploring is how you impact on others when you are in a negative state.

You will have been around people who let things get to them and are feeling negative. What's that like for you? Uncomfortable? Painful? Awkward? Embarrassing? However it impacts on you...the person creating this situation has no idea what they're doing to you or others. They are far too wrapped up in what's going on for them!

So how often do you create this situation for others? Go on, be honest. Remember that you won't be noticing the reaction of others...you'll just be noticing your own.

Recently, I was working with a team of sales managers and one of them openly admitted that her state first thing in the morning was awful. She had a 2 hour journey at best and felt jaded when she arrived at the office and really angry if her journey didn't go smoothly.

Her team reacted by not talking to each other, not talking to her and any positivity was generally flattened until her mood changed around 30 minutes later.

Everyone had got so used to the situation it was treated as the norm. In fact it had become an in-house joke.

Once she realised the impact on the team and on sales she was really committed to doing something about it and used these techniques to completely change her state...the impact on her team was enormous. They were more willing to come to her for help and guidance. Morale and confidence increased.

So it's really important to create a positive internal state in others in order to get the best levels of rapport. This in turn leads to better relationships and more co-operation...and that's just at work. Think about the positive impact when you apply this approach to your clients and prospects?

Remember...everything you do has an impact. So make sure it's a great one!

Change your state in a heartbeat

Sometimes you need a little extra help when it comes to improving your inner state. It may not always be that you're in a negative state because of something that has happened. It may be that you are unresourceful because of something that's coming up...maybe a big sales presentation or speaking at an event.

I love how the mind works in this situation. You can be the most confident person most of the time and yet your confidence has the ability to run and hide in the darkest corners of your mind when doing something new or outside your comfort zone.

One of my favourite Einstein quotes "Thinking puts boundary conditions around the limitless boundlessness that is you" is so true in this case. Add some thinking, a little nerves and uncertainty and you really can paralyse yourself.

Whatever it is that puts you in an unresourceful state, take heart because you can give yourself any resource...in a heartbeat!

You may have come across 'anchoring' before. Let me explain. Basically it's a technique that allows you to take the confidence you feel when you're at your best and resurrect it when you are not. Not just confidence either. You can use this technique for any state you need, for any situation.

Anchors are really powerful and you already have plenty of them. Think of a familiar food smell from your childhood...really associate to the experience. What emotions come up for you? Are you transported back there? Do your taste buds spring into action?

Think about a special song...or your most embarrassing moment ...or your biggest sales success. Notice your reactions when you really associate into the event. It's like you are back there in that moment...experiencing those emotions all over again.

You can now identify how these smells or songs transfer you quickly to where you associate them to.

Now think about it in the context of sales success. Imagine being able to conjure up confidence, determination, calmness or anything else you need at will...whenever you need it. It's really simple to do. You literally anchor past events in your life where they were at their peak.

My preferred anchoring technique is the Circle of Excellence. It's so easy and fun and works with everyone!

Give it a try when you want to be at your very best.

Circle of Excellence

Think of a resource you would like to have available to you in the future. This can be confidence, calmness, determination...absolutely anything. Think back to a time when you had this resource in the past. Associate a colour with that state.

Imagine an invisible circle on the floor in front of you. Make it about 3 feet in diameter and 2 feet in front of you. Make it the colour of your choice. Now add whatever you'd like into the circle that represents or supports the state you want to access. Do whatever you need to do so that your circle is as perfect as it can be.

Think of situations in the past where you have had huge amounts of the very resource you want to access. See yourself in the circle being magnificent and exhibiting these qualities. Really associate into the situation from your past. What are you doing; what are you saying; how are you feeling?

Put at least 3 resourceful events into your circle.

When you have built up your circle, step into it and experience the feeling of having that resource again here and now.

Step out of the circle.

Check with yourself...do you need to add anything to your circle?

Step back into the circle and notice how you feel again.

Really ramp up the feeling. Imagine you have a dial that increases the intensity and turn it up as much as you can stand.

Pick up your circle and put it somewhere that you can access...maybe an imaginary pocket. You can call it your resource pocket...and know that you have access to it whenever you need it.

You can add additional resources simply by throwing down your circle and going through the process again adding more of what you want.

To Summarise

In this chapter you've discovered what puts you in a positive state and what triggers your negative states. You've also got an excellent anchoring tool that allows you to access your inner resources at will.

What are your three priority actions that you're going to take as a result of reading this chapter?

1 ....

2 ....

3 ....

Go do them as quickly as you can

...anytime **NOW** would be good.

Leigh Ashton

5

Managing your Inner Software to Achieve More Sales

"Look within! The secret is inside you."

— Hui-neng

Your inner software

So far you've learned about the barriers that get in the way of your success, How to understand them, control them and reframe them to make yourself more resourceful internally.

Now it's time for you to explore the wonderful world of your inner software. The stuff that causes you to behave as you do. By understanding these programmes you will uncover what makes you tick, how you are motivated, how you absorb information and so much more.

You will also be able to recognise them in others which means you'll be able to tweak your approach with clients and prospects and increase your sales results.

It's such a big subject that I've split it into two parts. The first part covers how you process and store information and the second explores your inner patterns.

Part 1

How you process

Everything that happens around you is absorbed using your five senses: sight, sound, touch, taste and smell. This is how you store information in order to access it in the future. These are called Representation Systems.

Whilst you use all the senses to make sense of things you will have a preference for one...and this preference manifests itself in your thinking and the language you use. It is unlikely to be taste or smell as these systems are not multi dimensional enough.

So what's your preference and how does it impact on you. Let's start with a simple questionnaire to find out.

Representational Systems Profile Questionnaire

To provide you with a sense of your preferred representational system complete the following exercise:

For each question, write a 4 next to the phrase which best describes you, a 3 next to the phrase that would next best describe you and so on down to 1

I make important decisions based on:

A .... gut level feelings

B .... which way sounds the best

C .... what looks best to me

D .... precise and diligent study of the issue

During an argument, I am most likely to be influenced by:

A .... the other person's tone of voice

B .... whether or not I can see the other person's point of view

C .... the logic of the other person's arguments

D .... whether or not I feel I am in touch with the other person's true feelings

I most easily communicate what is going on with me by:

A .... the way I dress

B .... the feelings I share

C .... the words I choose

D .... my tone of voice

It is easy for me to:

A .... find the ideal volume and tuning on a stereo system

B .... select the most intellectually relevant points concerning an interesting subject

C .... select superbly comfortable furniture

D .... select rich colour combinations

I am very:

A .... attuned to the sounds in my surrounding

B .... adept at making sense of new facts and figures

C .... sensitive to the way articles of clothing feel on my body

D .... responsive to colours and the way a room looks

Insert your scores for each set of responses against the corresponding letters:

Response	Visual	Kinaesthetic	Auditory	Auditory Digital
1	C	A	B	D ....
2	B	D	A	C ....
3	A	B	D	C ....
4	D	C	A	B ....
5	D	C	A	B ....
Totals	....	....	....	....

The scores above indicate your relative preferences for each of the representational systems.

Representational System Traits

So now that you know what your preferences are, let's tell you about the traits.

If you scored highest for visual

You are most likely to stand or sit with your head and/or body upright, with your eyes up. You will be breathing from the top of your lungs. You often sit forward in your chair and tend to be organised, neat, well-groomed and orderly. You memorise by seeing pictures and are less distracted by noise. You often have trouble remembering verbal instructions because your mind tends to wander. You are more interested in how things look and appearances are important to you. You often speak very quickly when trying to keep up with the pictures in your mind...especially when you're excited. You're more likely to use phrases like...I see what you're saying, that looks good, get the picture.

If you scored highest for auditory

Your eyes will probably move from side to side when processing information and you will breathe from the middle of your chest. You generally speak slower than someone with a visual preference and typically talk to yourself...and may even move your lips when you do. You are easily distracted by noise. You find it easy to repeat things back and memorise by steps, procedures and sequences. You learn by listening, and usually like music and talking. You like to be told how you are doing and respond to a certain tone of voice or set of words. You will be interested in what others have to say. You're more likely to use phrases like...I hear where you're coming from, that sounds good, that rings a bell.

If you scored highest for kinaesthetic

You are more likely to breathe from the bottom of your lungs with your stomach going in and out when you breathe. You often move and talk verrry slowwwly and respond to physical rewards and touching. You like to feel comfortable in your clothes. You are also more likely to stand closer to people than the other preferences. You memorise by doing or walking through something and you will be interested in something only if it "feels right". You will often find yourself looking down when processing your thoughts. You're more likely to use phrases like...I'm comfortable with that, that feels right, I can get to grips with that.

If you scored highest for auditory digital

You will be more logical in your thinking with the need for things to make sense. You will spend a fair amount of time talking to yourself while you make sense of things and often find yourself looking down when processing. You will stone wall ideas if they don't make sense to you and others may perceive you as difficult in these situations. Once the penny drops, you find it easy to communicate across all preferences...and your scores may have reflected this. You're more likely to use phrases like...this doesn't make sense to me, that reasonable, that's not rational.

Now that you know what your preference is you can really make it work for you. If you are visual surround yourself with images to inspire and motivate, learn from others by watching what they do, write things down that are important to remember, in fact any visuals will work for you.

If you are auditory have some inspiring music or speeches that you can listen to easily to inspire and motivate. Talk to people you want to learn from and use good open questions to elicit as much of their knowledge verbally as you can.

If you are kinaesthetic have lots of tactile objects around you, be comfortable and practice lots to get new techniques in the muscle.

If you are auditory digital ask lots of questions in order to make sense of things in your mind so that you can progress.

Remember that you use all these Representational Systems but you will have a preference for one more than the others.

> From the age of 3 my niece Rema has been able to remember the names of everyone she comes into contact with...even if she only met them briefly. She would ask me where these people were by name weeks later. That really impressed me. She remembers everything she hears. Knowing this makes it really easy for me to know how to communicate with her...she loves to hear it!

Whatever you're preference it's really important to match the map of the client or prospect you are talking with to generate the deepest possible levels of rapport. You will truly be in their map if you tweak your approach to suit their world of communication.

Find out the preferred representational systems of all your contacts by asking good open questions...then really listen to the answers to pick up the language they use. Remember to incorporate the way they absorb information when communicating with them. A two way conversation is the prime objective but if you can't achieve that then use emails and texts for visuals; verbal messages for auditory and auditory digital or pop something in the post that a kinaesthetic can touch. You'll be helping them to receive your message and you'll connect with them at a much deeper level strengthening the relationship...and ultimately close more sales!

These following word examples will easily help you to identify the preferences of others:

Representational System Words

Visual	Auditory	Kinaesthetic	Auditory Digital
Analyse	Announce	Active	Change
Angle	Articulate	Affected	Conceive
Appear	Audible	Bearable	Consider
Aspect	Boisterous	Callous	Decide
Clarity	Communicate	Charge	Distinct
Cognisant	Converse	Concrete	Experience
Conspicuous	Discuss	Emotional	Insensitive
Demonstrate	Dissonant	Feel	Know
Dream	Divulge	Firm	Learn
Examine	Earshot	Flow	Logic
Focus	Enunciate	Foundation	Motivate
Foresee	Gossip	Grasp	Process
Glance	Hear	Grip	Question
Hindsight	Hush	Hanging	Reasonable
Horizon	Inquire	Hassle	Sense
Idea	Interview	Heated	Statistically
Illusion	Listen	Hold	Think
Illustrate	Loud	Hunch	Understand
Image	Mention	Hustle	
Inspect	Noise	Intuition	
Look	Oral	Lukewarm	
Notice	Proclaim	Motion	
Obscure	Pronounce	Muddled	
Observe	Remark	Panicky	
Obvious	Report	Pressure	
Outlook	Ring	Rush	
Perception	Roar	Sensitive	

Visual	Auditory	Kinaesthetic
Perspective	Rumour	Set
Picture	Say	Shallow
Pin-Point	Screech	Shift
See	Shrill	Softly
Scene	Silence	Solid
Scope	Sound	Sore
Scrutinise	Speak	Stir
Show	Speechless	Stress
Sight	Squeal	Structured
Sketchy	State	Support
Survey	Talk	Tension
Vague	Tell	Tied
View	Tone	Touch
Vision	Utter	Unbearable
Watch	Vocal	Unsettled

Part 2

Meta Programmes

For me...this is probably the most important area of your psychology to understand. These go deeper than Representational Systems because they are the unconscious filters that make up your personality. They determine the way you process information and formulate your patterns of behaviour...and how you operate in the world.

By understanding Meta Programmes you will be able to develop your awareness to understand and develop yourself and to predict and influence other people's behaviour; how they are motivated and how they make decisions. As you elicit a person's Meta Programmes, you will find out how they do what they do (inside) and this means you'll be able to communicate in a way that's perfect for them, establishing deeper levels of rapport more quickly and therefore making a positive impact with what you say.

Brief Background

Much of the initial work on Meta Programmes was undertaken by Leslie Cameron-Bandler in the USA and it was one of her students, Rodger Bailey, who first adapted and used her work within the context of business. Bailey also developed a series of questions that elicit a person's Meta Programmes, to create the Language and Behaviour Profile (LAB Profile). This has been popularised over recent years by Shelle Rose Charvet, author of "Words that Change Minds" (1995).

Different theorists identify different Meta Programmes e.g. Bodenhammer and Hall in "Figuring out People" identify 51 Meta Programmes, whereas O'Connor and Seymour in

"Introducing Neuro-Linguistic Programming" identify only seven categories. In some cases different labels are given to the same or similar programmes... match/mismatch equates to similarity/difference.

I'm going to give you my take on what I believe to be the major Meta Programmes that impact on Personal Development and Sales Success.

Context Dependent

It's really important to remember that Meta Programmes are context dependant and may change in different situations. For example, the way you behave in a personal relationship may be different to the way you act in relation to your work colleagues or customers.

Your Meta Programmes may also change over time as a result of specific significant emotional events.

Imagine the following Meta Programmes as being a continuum and that your preference can be at either end or at any point along it.

Understanding Meta Programmes

1. Towards & Away From

Answer the following questions with your immediate response...even if it doesn't make sense to you.

What do you love most about sales?

....

....

....

Why is that important to you?

....

....

Why is that important to you?

....

....

Why is that important to you?

....

....

(You need to have responses.)

You have just discovered whether you have a towards or away from preference in the area of sales (remember that you may have a different preference in other contexts)

So what's your preference? More on that after we explore some background!

You are motivated by only two things; pain and pleasure. You will constantly seek to reduce one and maximise the other.

Think of an outcome you want in either the short or the long term, what makes this outcome so attractive to you? What will achieving this outcome do for you? Will it give you pleasure or will it move you away from pain and discomfort?

Ask yourself how you came to be in your current job. Do you think it's because you were unhappy in your old job or do you think this job has all the qualities you wanted?

How did you come to buy your current car? Was it because you were dissatisfied with your old car or did you decide that this was the one for you because...?

If you are thinking that "moving towards" is positive and therefore good and "away from" is negative and bad, think again. Imagine being in a burning building - it might be useful to have a moving away from strategy here.

Like other Meta Programmes, towards and away from are just ways of being and are neither good nor bad.

Depending on the circumstances, one strategy might be more useful or appropriate than another. When setting your sales goals it's far better to move towards what you want than away from what you don't want.

If you want to give something up, by knowing your preference you can enhance your ability to increase your willpower. If you tend to move towards what you want, think of the benefits you'll get when you've given up. That's going to be far more motivating for you. If you have an away from preference you need to focus on the consequences if you don't. This will really drive you to move away from what you don't want.

Influencing Strategy with your clients and prospects

To motivate someone who is moving towards, you should emphasise their goals and outcomes, promoting the benefits of your offering, and letting them know you will help them get what they want.

To motivate a person who is moving away from, you should establish the problems and issues they don't want and really associate them into the consequences of doing nothing. Emphasise that you can help them to avoid what they don't want. Identify any potential problems and reassure them that these can be reduced or eliminated.

Back to you

So are your answers towards or away from to the three 'why' questions. Did you answer what you want or what you don't want?

Write down your preference in the context of sales here:

....

....

2. Internal & External

Answer the following question with your immediate response...even if it doesn't make sense to you.

How do you know you've done a good job?

....

....

....

Your response if you are externally referenced will be something like...you will know because someone tells you either verbally or non verbally...or you get a specific result like hitting your target.

On the other hand, if you are internally referenced your response will be that you just know...

Feedback comes from two sources...either from others or from you. If you don't believe or trust your own feedback you will need feedback from others to be sure that you're doing a good job.

When I train sales people in perfecting their presentations I ask them after their presentation to give me their view on one thing they did really well and one thing they could improve. Externally referenced people will find it easy to give me a number of things they could improve but only after pushing them do they give me one passable thing they did...just before asking me "what do you think?" This is because they need an external opinion to confirm what is good.

If you're internally referenced you will just know if you've done a good job as long as your outcomes are clear at the start. If you are not told what specifically is required, you will make up your own mind about what constitutes good performance. This may not be what the other person wants!

In setting goals for yourself it's good to be internally referenced. If a coaching client comes to me with sales goals that their manager wants them to achieve, I tell them to come back when they want to achieve them!

Influencing Strategy with your clients and prospects

To get your message across to an internally referenced person, set out all the information then get them to internalise it by asking "How would this work for you?" Use statements like "only you can know if this is right for you". They are not generally influenced by case studies and testimonials.

An externally referenced person is more influenced by case studies, testimonials and other businesses in their sector that use your services or products. The more you give them, the more they are reassured that they are making the right decision.

Back to you

So are you internally or externally referenced?

Write down your preference in the context of sales here:

....

....

3. Options & Procedures

Answer the following question with your immediate response...even if it doesn't make sense to you.

Why did you choose your current job?

....

....

....

If you have a procedural preference you are likely to say that they saw the job online, applied for it, went for an interview and go on to tell the story of how it happened...even though the question is 'why'. If you have an options preference you will have responded to the questions with the criteria or reasons you chose your job.

If you are procedural you will follow orders, requests and instructions to the letter. You will often get so caught up in how to do a task that you sometimes forget why you are doing it. You will often refer to "the right way" to do things. On the other hand, if you have an options preference you will want to experiment and continually ask "what if?" or "what else could we do?" questions. You sometimes seem compelled to be inventive and explore all the options.

In the past sales people have been taught to learn and work to scripts. Procedural people are great at this whilst options people will always seek to change the script in some way. What do you normally do?

As with all Meta Programmes there isn't a right or wrong way to be. It's all about appropriateness. Sometimes it will serve you to be procedural in terms of achieving your specific sales Key Performance Indicators (these will be specific to your organisation and can include criteria like...the number of meeting you generate and/or attend, how many meetings generate a proposal, how many proposals are converted into sales). Being procedural gets things done. Sometimes it's beneficial to explore all possibilities using an options approach rather than sticking to the process. This expands your thinking and gives you more choices.

There can be friction when options and procedural people get together. "I don't want to do it that way." "Well that's the way it should be done". My view is that diversity is the road to perfection and that there are times when both preferences are useful.

Influencing Strategy with your clients and prospects

When you interact with a procedural person you need to pay attention to the information you give, be exact and unambiguous. They will like clear cut steps...preferably those that are already tried and tested. Bear in mind they are likely to follow what you say verbatim. They need to know exactly how the relationship will go and what happens at every stage.

Give options people a couple of choices. Give them too many options and they get stuck knowing what to choose. Clearly set the boundaries, the musts and constraints. Emphasise various possibilities and let them know that the decision to buy will expand their choices. Then stand back and watch the results!

Back to you

So do you have an options or procedural preference?

Write down your preference in the context of work here:

....

....

4. Sameness & Difference

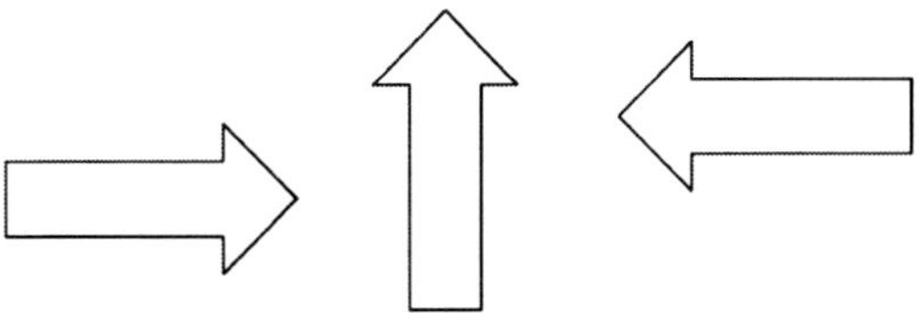

What's the relationship above?

What do you notice first; their similarities or their differences? Do you focus on what matches or what mismatches?

When you think about buying a new suit for work...how do you think about it? Do you think about getting one like the one so and so is wearing....or do you think about getting one that's different from the one that so and so has? Think of something you wear which you really like - do you like it because it's like....or because it's different from.....?

When you meet someone for the first time do you find yourself noticing how similar they are to someone else? Or maybe you notice how different this person is? How does your current job relate to what you were doing five years ago? Do you focus on the similarities or the differences? How about your current car...how does it relate to your previous one? Is it the same make or is it totally different?

If someone gives you some information do you accept it (yes, that's similar to what I thought) or do you challenge it (that can't be right, that's strange...). When you go through a proposal with a prospective client notice who says "that's a good idea" as opposed to "that won't work because..."

Increase your repertoire - if you filter for sameness, learn to filter for difference occasionally - challenge ideas and assumptions (you might begin by filtering your own internal dialogue, it's safer!). If you have a difference preference why not act as if you had a sameness preference when this might be appropriate - that would be OK, would it not?

Influencing Strategy with your clients and prospects

To really match a person with a sameness preference begin by helping them identify commonalities and similarities before moving on to how your service or product is better. When talking about the differences, frame them as small, gradual and evolutionary.

When interacting with a person with a difference preference... talk about newness, uniqueness and how your product or service is different from things they have tried before. Introduce commonalities and similarities casually in order to keep their focus on the differences.

Back to you

So do you focus on sameness or difference?

Write down your preference in the context of work here:

....

....

5. Proactive & Reactive

Are you the type that never seems to stop...or do you respond to things as they happen?

Are you thinking of or starting the next activity before you finish what you're doing? If your activity isn't prompted by anything particular other than your desire to get it done you will have a proactive preference.

If you might be equally as busy but responding to things around you like answering emails, returning phone calls, completing reports that your boss wants or the like then you have a reactive preference.

If you're proactive you'll initiate things and are always keen to start something new. You don't wait for others to initiate stuff.

You will use direct and positive language like "I shall begin by outlining the agenda for the meeting"

Clearly, the best sales people are likely to be proactive...just because you guys just get things done.

If you're reactive and you're left to your own devices, you will probably take a long time deciding what to do...and may never actually take action at all!

Your language will be more tentative and you'll seek to qualify what you say "If it's OK with everyone, I think I might begin the meeting by ...."

The opposing extremes of this Meta Programme can really create conflict. Often I'll go into an organisation with proactive, go getting people who are constrained by an underlying reactive culture. The people want to get things done but are prevented by rules, red tape, financial constraints and procedures. This is such a source of dissatisfaction...the people are employed because they have a proactive nature but then find that the company culture, regardless of what's said turn out to be reactive.

Influencing Strategy with your clients and prospects

The proactive customer will buy because they like what they see and want it. Just show them something they like and they'll go for it. Put your effort into bringing your service or product to their attention, give them the benefits and observe them get into buying mode!

The reactive buyer is likely to have already identified a need, thought it through, and maybe still be undecided. They will prefer to carefully weigh up all the possibilities, ask others for their opinion and only decide when pushed by deadlines. The best approach is to give them time to consider and a deadline for a decision.

Back to you

So are you proactive or reactive?

Write down your preference in the context of sales here:

....

....

6. Specific & General

Have you ever asked a client a question that can be answered in a sentence or two and they're still talking 10 minutes later?

Or maybe asked for more detail on a sales issue and been given a one line answer?

- Are you the person that is only interested in the big picture and give very brief responses regardless of the question...or do you give a very detailed response when a brief outline is all that's needed?
- Have you ever noticed that some people in your team or company complain that you're never given enough information about what's going on and others feel that you get too much information to digest?
- Some people only want a brief outline of the situation; others want to know every detail. Which one are you?

This can be a major source of frustration when the two preferences meet. The person with the general preference goes into shutdown when given too much information and the specific preference is dissatisfied with the level of detail they receive!

So what do you do?

You need to communicate to people around you the level of detail you want so that they can deliver. Don't expect people to know what you need!

Influencing Strategy with your clients and prospects

When you are communicating with your clients and prospects you absolutely must match their level of detail in order to stay in rapport. Too many details will confuse and irritate a general person and too much vagueness will upset the specific person. Give them the level of detail they need and check for understanding.

Back to you

So do you have a specific or general preference?

Write down your preference in the context of sales here:

....

....

7. Convincer Patterns

How do you become convinced to buy something? Do you just have to see it to know that you want it? If so how many times do you have to see it before you buy?

Your convincer pattern will work in two stages...the representation and the *demonstration*.

Representation

When making a decision to buy you will generally choose one of the following:

See	You need to see the item to know that you want it.
Hear	You need to hear about it from others.
Read	You need to read about it in a magazine
Do	You need to experience it... take a test drive or if it's a dress or suit, try it on

Demonstration

When are you convinced?

Automatic	You may be convinced straight away and may only need partial information.
Number of Times	You may need to experience the item on two or more occasions before you become convinced.
Time Period	You may need to experience the item consistently over a period of time before you buy.
Consistent	You may need to have information consistently every time to be convinced.

So how are you convinced about anything?

Do you have to see, hear, read or do in the first instance? What really hooks you in to start with?

Then how often do you have to...or is it a period of time for you? Or maybe you're never completely convinced?

Influencing Strategy with your clients and prospects

Understanding your clients and prospects convincer patterns makes it much easier to close the sale. Find out their pattern by asking about how they have decided to buy similar products or services in the past?

Be patient with the person that wants to see or hear about your offer several times over. The most challenging is the person with a consistent convincer as they will only be convinced by the last success at that time and doesn't have faith that it can be achieved again. The best option is to describe how it has proven consistently effective in the past.

Back to you

So what's your convincer pattern?

Write down your preferences in the context of work here:

Representation..

Demonstration...

To Summarise

This chapter has given you an understanding of your inner patterns and preferences and how to connect with others by recognising their preferences and tweaking your approach to better match their map of the world. This is definitely a chapter to read again and refer to.

What are your three priority actions that you're going to take as a result of reading this chapter?

1. ....

2. ....

3. ....

Go do them as quickly as you can

...anytime **NOW** would be good.

6 The Next Step

"The way to get started is to quit talking and begin doing."

—Walt Disney

Linking it together

If you're still with me well done! Five chapters in and my question is...

How much more do you know about yourself?

More importantly...what actions are you going to take to get you to where you want to go?

That's assuming you know where you want to go! So many sales professionals I come across have lack lustre goals. I want to reach target, I want to achieve the annual incentive or bonus, I want to progress, I want more money and the list goes on.

You can have wishes or you can have dynamic goals that really motivate you to reach for the stars.

When you have mediocre goals and let's face it, "I want to reach target" is pretty mediocre, you're setting yourself up to be ordinary not outstanding. What you really need to be doing is aiming for outstanding with some structure to get you there. You'll be discovering how to do that with the *Creating Dynamic Goals* exercise later in this chapter.

First of all let me tell you about my niece. She's 6 years old and has that wonderful quality that most children have of her age.

"Shyma can you sing?"

"Of course Auntie Leigh"

"Shyma can you dance?"

"Of course I can Auntie Leigh"

"Shyma can you bake cakes?"

"Of course Auntie Leigh"

"Of course Auntie Leigh...what was the question?"

Now let me tell you about my 15 year old nephew.

"Harry can you sing?"

"No way!"

"Harry can you dance?"

"A bit"

"Harry can you bake cakes?"

"No!"

It's wonderful to experience the curiosity and confidence of young children. They believe that everything is possible.

What do you think happens between the age of childlike innocence and the teenage years?

It's all about expectations. You don't get what you want in life you get what you expect. You start off expecting to achieve everything and in the main you achieve most of those things. It's the things you don't achieve that start to chip away at your expectations and take you to the mindset of better to aim low and not be disappointed.

I don't know where you are right now on your journey to success but what I do know is that most people that don't achieve the things they want in life have impotent goals. If you don't know where you're aiming, any road will do. You may get what you want by default but it certainly won't be by design.

Imagine being invited to a party and it's an address you haven't been to before. Do you leave the house with no idea how to get there or how much time you need to arrive on time...or to meet up with your friends? Of course not.

How often do you start work without clear goals for the day? What kind of day do you have if you don't set yourself clear goals?

Many years ago I went on a goal setting programme for my own development. I love being on the other side and putting myself in a learning state. I had a great time and came away with a list of actions I wanted to take. Somehow I lost my list...without even noticing. Several months later I found my action plan and when I looked at all the actions I'd planned I was very pleasantly surprised to find that I'd done all of them. Spooky? Not really. When you write down your goals you instruct your mind to find a way to do it.

Start by thinking about the things you really want to achieve? Think big. Dare to dream. How successful do you want to be? Really want to be? This isn't just about sales, it's about you. If you could star in your own epic movie, who would you be and what would you achieve? What kind of hero would you be?

Go find yourself a quiet and inspiring place with a notebook and write all your dreams and goals down. This won't be a five minute job so take your time and keep writing. When you think you're done...dig deeper and write more. When you think you're done for the second time, dig even deeper and write more. Go beyond two blank spots...this is often where you find the magic!

Before you read on, write up your goals and dreams taking all the time you need.

A goal in your mind is just a wish. You give energy to your goals when you write them down...and if you share them with someone that will support you...you'll be even more committed to achieving them.

In fact, having an accountability buddy will have a huge positive impact on your determination to succeed. Pick someone that you aspire to as a role model to raise the bar. Human nature is such that if you pick someone that has lower standards they will want you to stay there with them and put little seeds of doubt in your mind. They do it because they don't want to lose you or be left behind. Pick your buddy wisely!

Important Note: Always acknowledge that you are completely responsible for the achievement of your goals. As soon as you start blaming other people or the situation for your non achievement...you're in 'effect' and allowing yourself to be a victim.

Many of you will have come across SMART goals.

Specific

Measurable

Achievable

Realistic

Timed

Whilst it serves a purpose to cover a number of necessary criteria for goals, it misses some big chunks...and who in their right mind would want a realistic goal. Make your goals massive I say ☺ Be unrealistic!!!

I'm going to share with you a goal setting tool that I've been using for years and share with all my clients. You'll find this simple and easy to go through and it will give you a framework to achieve each of your goals and increase your motivation to achieve them.

Before you dive straight in with excitement and gusto, let me give you some pointers.

- Find yourself a quiet place where you won't be disturbed
- Give yourself plenty of time to answer all the questions
- Answer with complete honesty...your first reaction and response to each question is what you need to write down. Even if it doesn't make sense at the time...it will later!
- Your goal may change by the time you get to the end of the process...and that's fine
- Start with the goal that will make the biggest difference to your sales
- Your goal MUST be stated positively
- Ready, steady, off you go and create your dynamic goal...

Creating Dynamic Goals

Stated in the positive.

What do you want?

....

....

Evidence procedure in place

What would be your evidence that you have achieved your goal?

....

....

What would you be doing to get it?

....

....

What would you be seeing/hearing/feeling?

....

....

What would be a demonstration your achievement?

....

....

Appropriately specified and contextualised

Where do you want this goal?

....

....

Where do you not want this goal?

....

....

When do you want this goal?

....

....

When do you not want this goal?

....

....

With whom do you want this goal?

....

....

With whom do you not want this goal?

....

....

Self-initiated and maintained

What resources can you activate to get this goal?

....

....

What resources can you acquire to get this goal?

....

....

What can you do right now?

....

....

What can you continue doing?

....

....

Ecological

What will happen if you get this goal?

....

....

How will getting this goal affect other aspects of your life?

....

....

How does getting this goal benefit you?

....

....

What might you lose if it happens?

....

....

What's the first action you can take immediately?

....

....

Congratulations! Your first Dynamic Goal is set in motion

Increasing your commitment

There are a number of things you can do to really ramp up your success. One of my favourite techniques is to visualise the successful completion of my goal. I see myself having achieved my goal, full of happiness and joy. My visualisation is in full technicolour, really bright and vivid and I experience all the sounds and feelings to go with it.

A friend of mine, Ron Holland takes his visualisation a stage further. Many years ago he wanted his book published by a specific publisher in the States. Not only did he visualise that happening...he actually put on a suit, picked up his briefcase, drove to Heathrow and sat in the lounge watching planes and visualised himself through the whole thing from boarding the flight to walking into the publishers office. He visualised it every day and had 2 more visits to Heathrow before it happened for real.

Now that's what I call commitment!

Visualising works best when you do it on waking and before you go to sleep for around 5 minutes each time. More than that and your mind may start to drift. First of all see your experience through your own eyes...really associate into it. Experience all the emotions that make it perfect, then step out of your body and leave yourself in the picture...as if you are looking at a photograph or a movie of yourself. It must feel great to you or it won't have the impact. Keep tweaking it till it's as perfect as it can be. It's really important to visualise the successful completion of each goal rather than how you're going to achieve it. That will work itself out on its own!

Visualisation is a key component of the Law of Attraction. The theory is that you visualise the successful completion of the things you want to achieve in your life and leave the 'how it happens' to the universe...and the universe provides.

I have my own theory about why this approach works and it's this...your mind delivers what you focus on and because you're focusing on achievement, you are more likely to exhibit the behaviours and spot the opportunities that will lead you to achieve the things you desire simply because it's on your radar. The brain doesn't distinguish between reality and fantasy so if you visualise each day you're training your mind that this is all reality and it's only a question of time before it happens. You're reinforcing the positive elements that keep you motivated to take action towards the achievement of your visualisation!

However, what I can't explain is the simple act of mentally ordering a parking space before I leave to go somewhere busy...and then finding that space on arrival. That really is a mystery to me...but while it keeps working, I'm going to keep doing it. The Law of Attraction works in my map of the world!

You may also find *affirmations* are a useful addition to your motivation armoury. Repeatedly saying positive things about you, your capabilities and your goals loudly to yourself in a mirror on waking and before bed will definitely reinforce your positivity and your state.

Be sure to state what you want rather than what you don't want when using affirmations...you wouldn't want to be reinforcing negative messages would you!! Things like "I will be the top sales producer this month...I am confident when negotiating...I stay calm in all situations" can really add to your self belief. Craft the wording to really get your juices flowing!

Now you're really armed with some great tools to keep you on track. You've got your Dynamic Goals, you're visualising and using the Law of Attraction, you're using affirmations. Fantastic...what could possibly go wrong?

Procrastination!

Procrastination is a human trait that just creeps up on you. One minute you can be going like a train towards the achievement of your goals...then it happens. You notice that you're not following through on actions that you know will make a big difference. Pat yourself on the back that you've even noticed. Sometimes this goes on for ages before you realise...or someone points it out to you!

So what can you do when procrastination creeps in? I have a little technique that I want to share with you. This is great when you're procrastinating and need to get back on track towards your goals.

> I did this exercise recently with a team of recruitment consultants and one of them got really upset when answering the question 'What will it cost you if you don't make this change?' Her sales in the previous 3 months had been poor and the learning she got from this exercise allowed her to let go of the past and move forward. When I spoke to her boss the following week she had made 3 placements!

Here are some pointers before you start.

Find yourself a quiet place where you won't be disturbed.
Give yourself plenty of time to answer all the questions
You may feel pretty uncomfortable (I hope so) when considering the consequences of not making this change
You will feel completely inspired by the end of it

Are you ready to Commit to Action? Go for it...

Write down one thing that you are not following through on.

Come up with 10 reasons why you absolutely must change this now:

1. ....

2. ....

3. ....

4. ....

5. ....

6. ....

7. ....

8. ....

9. ....

10. ....

What will it cost you if you don't make this change?

....

....

What will you gain from this change?

....

....

Why do you know you can absolutely make this change?

....

....

Create a new association with this change?

Make it perfect for you!

Example: If you're not making enough calls you may have an association that not making calls equals less rejection...a new association might be that making more calls equals more chances to develop relationships that generate sales and all the kudos and success that comes with it.

This is really important. You must create a new association. Do not proceed until you have created one!

....

....

....

....

What's your first action that you can do immediately?

....

....

Congratulations! Go do your first action right now.

To Summarise

In this chapter you've discovered some tools to help you create goals that you're really motivated to achieve, how to stay positive on the journey and how to deal with procrastination.

What are your three priority actions that you're going to take as a result of reading this chapter?

1 ....

2 ....

3 ....

Go do them as quickly as you can

...anytime **NOW** would be good.

7
Modelling Sales Success

"The quality of a person's life is in direct proportion to their commitment to excellence"

—Vincent Lombardi

Find yourself a great strategy

Have you ever wondered why some people are able to exceed sales targets easily and consistently and others try really hard and don't get the same level of success?

It's all down to strategies! When you do things brilliantly and effortlessly it means you have developed a great strategy. When you struggle it means you have an ineffective strategy. You have millions of strategies. You'll have one for getting up in the morning. You'll have one for preparing your meals. You'll have one for your journey to work...the list goes on. You have devised a strategy for everything you do.

So what is a strategy exactly? In this context it's the precise...and I mean precise...order and sequence of what you think and do from the trigger point to completion of the specific activity. Every thought you have during the process impacts on your inner state and behaviour. Just to make it interesting, there are elements of your strategies that are done completely unconsciously!

You have modelled other people's strategies from the moment you were born. You watched and copied what you saw and in no time you were walking, talking, dancing and feeding yourself! You would have been thrilled every time you mastered a new strategy...and it's exactly the same as an adult. Think of it...all the things in your life that aren't as you'd like...and changing them easily by modelling yourself on a person that has successfully done what you want to achieve!

Some of your strategies work well consistently over time...and some strategies become out of date. The problem you'll have is that you don't always realise they are out of date and continue to use them.

A consultant friend of mine told me a story that's a great example of the importance of measuring the success of the strategies you are using.

> He was working with a company many years ago and was curious to find out why the words on internal memo's didn't go any further than two thirds down the page before starting the next sheet. He asked lots of people and nobody seemed to know how this practice had developed. All staff had been instructed to do it this way and had never questioned it. Eventually he found the answer. Many years earlier a photocopier had developed a fault and only copied the top two thirds of each page. What a great strategy they devised. It worked perfectly then.

If you aren't getting the sales results you want, my guess is you've got some strategies that just don't work for you. In fact once you start scrutinising them you'll probably find that some of your strategies are actually making it more difficult for you to achieve the sales success you want.

So the secret to being an amazingly successful sales professional is to carry on using your strategies that deliver results and ditch the ones that don't...and in their place you put proven strategies you know will get you the results you want. How do you know? You go and find someone that is already achieving the results you want and elicit their strategy so that you can use it yourself!

There are some pointers to consider before you go charging off in pursuit of the most successful sales person you can find. You must find someone that gets the exact result you want and behaves and thinks in a way that you would be happy to model.

For you to get the same result you will need to do exactly what they do...so choose your person wisely!

When you find your person – it's not just what you see in terms of behaviours that you need to elicit. Think of their strategy as an iceberg and their behaviours as the bit you see above the water line. Nine tenths of an iceberg is below the water line and it will be in this part of their strategy, where the magic is.

You will need to decide exactly which part of their strategy you want to model. Say you want to improve your presentation skills. There are a number of strategies that make up a presentation: like assessing the right level of information; how each topic flows; how you construct your handouts; connecting with your audience in the first 2 minutes; closing the presentation...and so on. Be very clear in your own mind which bit you want to go for and if you want the whole thing, break it down into manageable chunks. The person you model will have a string of strategies that make up what you want to replicate.

Remember that you may already have a number of skills that make up the strategy you want to model and that by changing a couple of things you'll take your performance from OK to excellent.

Ready? Let's get started.

The Five Key Elements

There are 5 key elements to modelling a person's strategy:

The behaviour you see

This is the part of the iceberg that you can see. Sometimes just by watching you can pick up enough information to get you started. That's how you would have learned as a child...mimicking everything you saw and heard.

Physiology

Your mind and body are totally linked. The way you move your body, your muscles tone and tension, the way you breathe, your facial expressions and posture all impact on your inner state. Your state then determines the quality of your behaviours.

You need to establish exactly how the person uses their physiology when they're carrying out the strategy you want to model.

Thinking strategies

You have thoughts in a very specific sequence when you do things. Your thoughts are made up of the information that comes in through your five senses and words you use to describe your experience.

Pay lots of attention to the pictures people make in their minds, the sounds they hear...especially the things they say to themselves, and the feelings they have when they're performing the skill you want to learn. All these are crucial in reproducing the result you want.

Beliefs

What you believe about a skill or behaviour will have a significant effect on your performance. If you have a belief that talking to an audience of 200 people is exciting, then you're going to perform very differently to if you have a belief that it's the most terrifying thing you could possibly have to do.

Taking on the beliefs of a person achieving the success you want is an important part of the process. You must feel completely at ease to take on the beliefs this person holds.

Values

Your values are core to who you are. When your values are being met you're happy. You'll know all about it when someone violates your values!

If your values when writing stuff on a flip chart is to capture *all the relevant information*...then that won't satisfy a person whose values are *the minimum amount of information be presented, using different colours and the writing straight across in lower case!*

So find out what's really important to the person you're modelling when they are carrying out the skill you want. Elicit the finer distinctions.

How you learn

You will have a preferred learning style which makes it really easy to pick up certain information...and more challenging to pick up others. You will have a tendency to elicit your preferred elements based on your style and it is crucial that you pick up all the parts of the strategy. The person you're modelling will also have more awareness of the parts of their strategy that fall under their preference. You'll need to get beyond both of your preferred strategies to get a complete process to follow.

> I've been modelled on a number of occasions by people wanting to replicate my skills and it's been a fantastic experience for me too. Not only am I contributing to the other person's success which is of high value for me...I'm also finding out what I do at an unconscious level when I'm in flow and doing what I do best. So remember that modelling a person's strategy is a two way street with both sides benefitting enormously!

There are, however four learning styles for you to be aware of when eliciting a strategy.

'Why' Learners

If this is you, you're likely to question the 'what' and the 'reasons' behind things. You can be quite irritating by asking lots of questions to satisfy your own desire to know rather than sticking to what's important. Asking 'why' questions will elicit a person's values so be mindful not to trample on them. You are often too quick with assumptions and have a tendency to impose your own map. When modelling...it's the other person's map that's important.

'What' Learners

If this is you you'll love information. You'll want as much as you can get and may be distracted by irrelevant information rather than the finer distinctions. For example, when a person is explaining what they see you may well be happy identifying what they see but you need to ask them if they are associated and looking through their own eyes or dissociated and looking at themselves when they are making pictures in their minds?

Be aware that receiving lots of information on process isn't getting the strategy so beware!

'How' Learners

If this is you you'll love the 'how it's done'. You're probably impatient and want to get on and 'DO' before you've got all the information. There could be a tendency to irritate by acting as if you've got it and know the skill better than the person you're modelling. Take the time, ask the questions and really listen!

'What if' Learners

If this is you you'll probably want to check lots of examples outside of the strategy you're eliciting. This can really scramble the other persons thinking by directing them here, there and everywhere. The danger here is that they lose their thread and can't give you what you need. Keep them associated into the specific skill to get the best results.

Planning your strategy session

What strategy do you want?

What specific skill do you want? Remember that a person's capabilities are made up of a number of skills and you need to be specific about which skill you want to model. There could be a number of them...do one session for each skill. Start with the skill that will have the biggest impact on your sales success.

Who's the right person?

Who do you know that has the skill you want and carries it out in a way that you can replicate? If you don't know them personally, get an introduction. Most people are flattered and very willing to help when they're asked. Pick the person with an outstanding strategy that consistently delivers excellent results and not someone who is just OK at the skill. Tell them what you plan to do and answer any questions they have before the session.

Strategy overview

Get a general and relatively brief understanding of the skill and how they do it. How it begins and ends, what, where, when and how...and in what sequence.

Strategy detail

Get more and more detail on how the skill is carried out at each stage of the process. Get the person to really associate in by carrying out the skill...even if it's only in their imagination. This makes it much easier for them to access the fine detail even they may not be aware of.

Check your understanding

Throughout the session keep checking that you're on the right track with your understanding. Remember to focus on the skill rather than the capability.

Try the skill

The test that you've elicited the complete strategy is to perform the skill yourself...and get the same result! Celebrate and give the person a big hug.

Great strategy elicitation questions

The quality of your questions will determine the quality of your strategy elicitation. The better your elicitation, the better you're able to replicate the strategy.

Use the following questions to elicit the key elements of a strategy.

Behaviour

- When do you use this skill?
- How do you know when to use this skill?
- What happens first?
- What happens next?
- What else happens at this point?
- What do you do next?
- How do you know that you have finished?
- When do you stop?
- What else is relevant?

Physiology

- What sensations are you aware of when you're performing this skill?
- How do you hold your body?
- What's your rate of breathing?
- What else do you notice?

Thinking

- What do you see?
- What do you hear?
- What do you say to yourself?
- What do you feel?

Beliefs

- What would happen if you did...?
- What would happen if you didn't...?
- What makes you...?
- What stops you...?
- What does doing this enable you to do?
- What does this make possible?
- What beliefs are at play here?

Values

- What is important to pay attention to?
- What's important to you about this?
- What are your criteria for this? Why is that important to you?

In addition, keep the following pointers in mind.

- Get the person to associate into the skill...be either doing it there and then or visualising themselves doing it so that you get all the detail
- Keep to the context of the skill that you want to model
- Be aware of your own patterns – before using theirs
- Run their strategy through your own mind at each stage
- Their internal processes are essential
- We all have different interpretations of words...use their words at all times
- Use it or lose it!!! Practice, practice, practice.

You now have everything you need to elicit and replicate a winning strategy. Have fun with this and increase your sales success by finding excellence in others. You don't have to reinvent the wheel if somebody has done it already!

So what would you like to do better?

Think of three skills that would really increase your success if you had a winning strategy?

1 ....

2 ....

3 ....

What people do you have access to (direct and indirect) that are excellent at these skills?

1 ....

2 ....

3 ....

4 ....

5 ....

6 ....

Make that call right now. The quicker you get this...the easier your sales success will come!

To Summarise

In this chapter you've discovered how to elicit a successful strategy in order to replicate the same results for yourself. You may find that when carrying out the strategy you've elicited for yourself it may not be totally comfortable and easy for you. This is perfectly OK. It will get easier each time you use the new strategy and before you know it you'll be using it as if it had been your own to start with.

What are your three priority actions that you're going to take as a result of reading this chapter?

1 ....

2 ....

3 ....

Go do them as quickly as you can

...anytime **NOW** would be good.

8 Measuring Up

"Action is the real measure of intelligence"

— Napoleon Hill

Key Performance Indicators

Assessing what you do and knowing what to tweak for greater impact will keep you on the path of continual improvement.

You should already be measuring your *Key Performance Indicators* (KPI's) to give you some facts on how effective you are. KPI's will vary from company to company but the common ones measured are the number of leads, meetings, proposals, conversions and value of orders or similar.

Now I know that paperwork may not be your favourite pastime as a sales professional but it really is essential to know how you're doing and will flag up where your best results come from and where your results don't warrant your input.

My view is that you should only measure yourself to the 'you' of yesterday. OK, someone else may be doing more meetings, proposals and conversions. You are not them. Establish where you are with your KPI's and pledge to improve them step by step. It's far better to improve a hundred things by one percent than to improve one thing by a hundred percent. Don't let the higher KPI levels of others effect your determination and motivation to improve your own.

Many years ago I had a team of telemarketing consultants that generated meetings for our clients. The daily call rate was generally between 70 -100 calls per day...except one consultant. Paul's call rate was around 38 calls per day. Shocking you may say. Not as effective as the other consultants you might add. Absolutely wrong! He had the highest meeting conversion rate of all the consultants.

If you try to push Paul to do more calls he loses an element of his strategy that's vital for his success. His and my measure of his effectiveness is through the increase in his results. Let that be your measure...not the number of the measure itself.

Regardless of the KPI's you currently measure...which ones do you want to improve? List them here:

1 ....

2 ....

3 ....

The 5 Keys to Sales Success

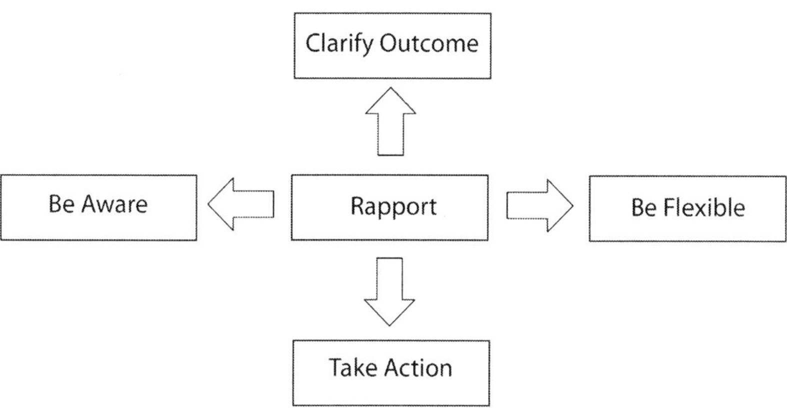

Take a look at the 5 Keys. They are all crucial elements to achieving success though there is an order and sequence in which you should use them.

When you look at all the mega successful people around you, have you noticed how different they all are? That's great news...it means that success can be achieved regardless of the preferences you have. You don't need to be a clone of someone you don't relate to.

There are certain things that are always evident though and the ability to apply the 5 Keys can be found in all successful people.

Of all the techniques I've learned along the way, this is the one I use most. Not only do I use it every day...I use it more than once a day. I use it to plan and to assess how I'm doing. For me it's a vital tool for everyone and an excellent addition to your sales toolbox.

1. Clarify your outcome

Always, always, always decide what you want to achieve. Without an end goal you are more likely to drift in all sorts of directions. You may get what you want by default but it won't be by design. To be in control you need to know what you want...and if you don't know what you want, how do you know when you've got to what you want?

Take a moment to think about your outcomes when you start work in the morning. If you've ever had an outcome like..."let's just get through the day with the least amount of pain and leave at 5pm"...then you probably won't be achieving too many sales. Focus on what you want to achieve by the end of the day and be specific. How many calls do you plan to make, how many meetings do you plan to book, how many sales do you plan to close? It's your choice. Remember you get what you focus on so focus on achieving exactly what you want and expect it to happen!

2. Take action

It doesn't matter how much you want something or how much you visualise a successful outcome...if you don't take any action it won't happen. In my experience most people fail because of a lack of action. Some of them know they're not taking action and others...well they keep themselves busy doing loads of stuff that isn't productive just to avoid the very action they need to take. Even though I don't know you, I'll take a guess that you can exercise both approaches. When you're really motivated you take action and get results and when you're not so motivated or confident you use all the avoidance strategies you can find!

In my book it's 'take action'...and any action will do. Even the wrong action get's you off the starting block. With that comes momentum and that's often all you need to get you on the right track.

You know what it's like...you need to make sales calls and you're not in the mood. You make the first one anyway and then you make the second and before you know it you're making your calls and in your stride.

When planning your sales outcomes for the day, add the actions you need to take to move you closer to achieving what you want.

3. Be aware

Are your actions taking you closer towards what you want...or further away?

When I work with sales teams that aren't performing I often find that they're taking action that may well have got results for them in the past...and even though these actions have stopped getting the results...they still keep doing them in the hope they will work again. They are not assessing the impact of their actions!

You and I live in a fast moving world that sales approaches need refining constantly. What you do this month may not work next month. What didn't work last month may work this month!

Increase your awareness of the results you're creating.

4. Be flexible

If you're not generating the sales you want then do something else...and keep doing something else until you get the results you want.

This is about how you react and manage the changing environment.

Increase your flexibility in thinking and action to reflect what's going on with your buyers. If what you're doing doesn't increase their desire to buy from you...find a way that does!

5. Rapport

You may have expected rapport to be the most important key and in many ways it is. It should be present in every interaction you have. Your ability to achieve the ultimate success depends on your ability to get into rapport. From the person that answers the phone when prospecting to the decision maker you want to reach, from the most junior person in your company up to your CEO...in fact everyone. In Hollywood they say..."Be nice to everyone on the way up because you never know who you'll meet on the way down" You have no idea how a person might impact on your success so connect with everyone in a positive way to increase your presence and success.

When you use The 5 Keys to Sales Success to plan, decide your outcome, plan your action steps, think about the potential results you might get from these actions and work on contingency plans if you first don't get the result you want. Think about how you can maintain rapport at every stage.

When you use The 5 Keys to Sales Success to assess, think about the original outcome, review the actions you took, establish what the results were, explore what you could have done differently to increase your success...and all in rapport of course. This will really help you to transform all your activity into winning strategies.

You can also use The 5 Keys to Sales Success when you are stuck in a position. Think of something that isn't working for you right now and run it through each stage by asking the following questions:

- What is your outcome?
- What action did you take?
- Did the action take you closer to your outcome or further away?
- What are the alternative actions you can take?
- How can you increase rapport?

When email tracking first hit the sales scene I was so excited to be able to see how many people opened our emails and even more excited about the number of people that clicked through for further information about our workshop. I was really happy with the percentages and was ready to celebrate until I remembered what my outcome for the email campaign actually was...and that was to generate bookings for a workshop I was running the following month. In that respect I had 2 bookings...so my joy was a little premature!

It's all very well celebrating success but be sure that it's the success you actually want or you may take your foot off the accelerator before you get to your destination.

Focus on your outcome at all times and use *The 5 Keys to Sales Success* to keep you on track.

There's no such thing as failure ...only feedback

Everything you do creates a result. Some results you love. Some results you don't. It's all feedback on how you're doing.

Imagine a world where the only feedback you received was that you are wonderful, brilliant and amazing! If that's all you ever heard from people what do you think would happen? You would probably become complacent and at best your results would plateau and at worst your results would go into decline.

You absolutely need feedback on the areas where you're not great. If nobody tells you...how are you going to improve it?

I don't know whether feedback features highly where you work but most people are only comfortable giving positive feedback. There's a skill in giving feedback that generates learning and development. Congratulations if you get feedback to help you grow your success...and thank the people that have the confidence to tell you.

If you don't get that kind of feedback...and in a way that makes it palatable then you need to instigate the feedback you need to grow your skills and your success.

You also need to accept it in the spirit of which it's meant. Getting all defensive and making excuses for why you did what you did won't get you very far. It will also put people off giving you what you need. Accept it graciously, thank them...then reflect. You haven't got to agree with them. Remember it's their feedback based on their map of the world. Consider though that if they have this perspective, others may too. If you can strengthen your strategies to get a positive response from a wider audience by considering this feedback then definitely incorporate it in your approach. You'll soon know if it improves your results or not!

When asking for feedback, be very specific with your questions to help the person help you. Asking "what do you think?" is too vague.

Some of my favourites are:

- What did you specifically like?
- What didn't work for you?
- What could I have done to make it better for you?
- Would you buy?

If you're not used to getting this kind of feedback and are a little unnerved by the responses you might get...get over it. This is the only way to continual improvement.

As a stepping stone you can use a self assessment questionnaire. Here's one that I've created to use after a meeting or telephone conversation. Ask yourself the questions and be completely honest...100%

The Outcome

Was I clear on my direction and focus throughout?

The Opening

How successful was I in opening the discussion?

The Rapport

Was the person at ease and able to talk freely?

Coverage

Did I collect all the information needed?
Did I impart all relevant information?

Detail

Did I collect information in sufficient detail?
Did I provide clear understandable information to the person?

Flow

Did the discussion flow smoothly from one topic to another, without awkward pauses?

Manner

Was I courteous, tactful, etc?
How did I show I was listening?

Question Technique

Did I ask open-ended questions and expand where necessary?
Did I ask leading questions or answer my own questions?
Did I talk too much?
Did I listen?

The Close

How successful was I in closing the discussion?
Does the person know what will happen next?
Did I achieve my outcome?

Not all these questions may apply in your situation so tweak it to make it work for you. Once you're comfortable with your own feedback, take the plunge and ask others. Remember that your feedback comes from your own perspective...and you have unconscious patterns that only others can help you identify.

Enjoy your feedback!

How to make changes

Once you have feedback you can decide what action you need to take to get you on track to achieving your sales goals. Sometimes you will know exactly what you need to do and that's great...just do exactly that. Use *The 5 Keys to Sales Success* to plan your approach and to assess the impact of your changes.

If you're not sure what to do, then find someone to help you. You don't know what you don't know and sometimes you need the spotlight focused on a possible solution by someone else. You can really learn from somebody that has been there, done that and got the T shirt! They don't have to work at the same organisation...unless you think that's an important element of the help you need. People outside of the organisation or situation often bring a fresh perspective that can be so useful in helping you decide the way forward.

When choosing a mentor make sure...

- You trust and respect them
- They operate in a way that's in alignment with your approach
- They have achieved success in the area you need help with
- It's someone you aspire to

It's all very well asking your colleagues for advice but be wary of asking people that are not achieving what you're striving for. You really don't want to be modelling lower standards and they will be more than happy to reassure you it's not your fault because it reinforces for them the reasons and excuses they have been giving themselves for their lack of performance.

If you're creative you may like an approach I use from time to time. I ask myself what advice I would get from a wide spectrum of people and beyond. Try it for yourself and see how you get on.

Think about the issue and ask yourself what advice you would get from...

- A mentor – living or dead, known or unknown to you
- A favourite comedian
- A young precocious child
- A favourite pet or animal
- An alien
- Yourself in 20 years time
- Yourself 20 years ago

Notice how the advice you get from each one affects your thinking on the issue. All will bring wisdom worth considering. Have fun with this and feel free to add more to the list!

Once you have decided on the action you need to take....TAKE THE FIRST STEP IMMEDIATELY!

Quantum questions

Quantum Questions are a useful tool for self exploration that help you increase awareness of your thoughts and definitions on issues that are demanding your attention.

These 4 very specific questions will really help you challenge your thoughts from different perspectives.

I remember working with a lady that really wanted to get into sales and couldn't make her mind up what to do. She was in a job that gave her the comfort of a great salary but wasn't giving her the challenge she wanted. Within 6 months not only had she found a sales job that she was happy in...she also was one of the top performers in the company. When asked she said that this session had caused her to understand everything that was involved...positive and negative...and to plan her approach with all that in mind.

Before I give you the four questions, start with the issue you want to address. Grab your notebook, find yourself a quiet place and give yourself plenty of time to answer the questions.

Keep writing for as long as you can then ask yourself "What else" and keep asking till you've absolutely exhausted the answers. You will know when you've got to a natural end because there will be no emotional charge left...a kind of flatness or neutral sense. Then one last time ask yourself "If there was one thing you may have forgotten...what would it be?"

Here are those magical questions.

- What would happen if you did?
- What would happen if you didn't?

- What wouldn't happen if you did?
- What wouldn't happen if you didn't?

These are so simple and will give you powerful insights that you're unlikely to get in any other way.

So take what you've discovered and make your plan!

To Summarise

In this chapter you've discovered how you can use KPI's to improve your performance, how to use The 5 Keys to Sales Success to plan, assess and keep you on track, the importance of feedback in your personal development, how to make changes and how Quantum Questions can help you to explore an issue to a very deep level.

What are your three priority actions that you're going to take as a result of reading this chapter?

1 ....

2 ....

3 ....

Go do them as quickly as you can

...anytime **NOW** would be good.

9 Putting it all Together

"Success is simple.
Do what's right, the right way, at the right time"

— Arnold H. Glasgow

There's something really important that holds all you've read in this book together and makes the magic happen when it comes to generating high levels of sales.

Rapport!

The ability to get into deep levels of rapport is what makes the difference between an OK sales person and an amazing one. When you use the techniques you've read in this book with your clients and prospective clients you will get better results if you focus on rapport rather than the technique itself. It's like fairy dust.

Remember that it's one of the 5 Keys to Sales Success...and it's there for a very good reason!

To recap on how to maximise rapport?

There really is only one way and that's to match the other persons map of the world to the greatest degree you can. The physical things are easy to match...physiology and voice. It's the preferences and patterns that really make the difference. Increase your awareness of their representational system and meta programme preferences and you will get a greater understanding of what they want and how you can best help them...and they will find you irresistible to connect with.

Over the years I've employed lots of sales professionals and I've observed two approaches. The people that focus on perfecting these techniques can sometimes get mixed results. It's the people that focus on rapport that get outstanding results every time! That's because when you are in rapport your sensory acuity is increased and you will pick up subtle distinctions that may alter the way you use the technique with the person you are with.

Open questions

Another point that holds this all together is the ability to ask great questions.

Closed questions are banned in my business. My belief is that they serve no purpose whatsoever. Firstly they give you very little information, the criteria comes from your map and the other person is either agreeing with you or not by their yes or no response and the worst part is that you don't get any dialogue using closed questions.

The language a person uses are the clues to what's going on inside them. They are the clues that allow you to understand the structure of their world and give you access to the information they don't necessarily verbalise directly.

Your open questions should start with any of the following:

What

How

Where

When

Who

All these create dialogue but the most useful are **WHAT** and **HOW** questions. The **WHAT** gives you the criteria that are important to the other person and the **HOW** gives you the processes they use. Both are really important when eliciting another person's map of the world.

When I first got into sales it was considered OK to use '**why**' questions...why did you choose the other supplier?...why didn't we get the business? Now that I understand psychology in sales and communication I absolutely know that 'why' questions are to be used with extreme caution.

Whenever you ask a 'why' question you are asking for justification of what's just been said...and that creates emotions in the other person that they need to defend their corner no matter what. You will get a response that is emotional rather than criteria based and that is of no use if you're to stand any chance of opening a discussion that may influence a positive outcome for you.

You may also jeopardise the rapport that you had before asking the question.

Think for a moment...what emotion comes up for you when you're asked "why did you do that?" Uncomfortable eh! So don't subject others to that when what you really want to do is develop your relationship in a positive way. Far better to ask "What is it about the other company that makes you think they are a better option?" or "What is it about our offer that is less than perfect?" The responses that you get to these questions will give you the criteria that you need to match to bring you closer to what the client wants.

Go find yourself a quiet corner and take some time to write as many open questions as you can. Focus on questions that really help you identify what's going on in the other person's map of the world so that you have a greater chance to tailor your offering to suit them exactly. Keep these questions with you at all times. Test them with clients constantly and tweak the ones that don't get you the results you want. Remember if you're not getting the information you want...ask better questions!

IPA

A really important attitude to apply in sales is IPA – *Income Producing Activity.* You will generate more sales if you focus your attention on activities that have a direct impact on creating sales opportunities. By this I mean activity prior to a sale being made. This could be prospect meetings, creating email campaigns, generating referrals...anything that starts or develops new relationships with prospective customers. What you do with your client after the deal has been done is around customer service and quality...and is *not* IPA. Now I know that it's important to keep clients happy and the happier you make them the more likely they are to buy again but any time you spend servicing the client doesn't count unless you are talking with them about another service or product that they might buy.

If you're filling your time talking to existing customers you'll feel like you're doing a great job but it won't generate the level of sales you want to be a top achiever. Leave customer service to your customer service team and if customer service is part of your role make sure that you spend between 1 - 3 hours every day on IPA.

So how much of your time is actually spent on IPA?

FBI

Many years ago I came across this acronym that I have used ever since. It is so simple and so effective I pass it on to everyone.

FBI - no it's not the Federal Bureau of Investigation, it's...

Fastest

Business

Impact

When I have a mountain of 'IPA' I could be doing, I ask myself what's the FBI here? This really helps me prioritise what's going to create the biggest impact on my sales...then I do that first. When I've completed that activity I ask myself again and do the next most important activity.

It's really easy to get caught up with doing stuff that doesn't create sales for you...especially when you're busy.

Keep on track by constantly checking in with yourself. Is this really the most important thing you could be doing? What level of impact does it have on your sales?

Think FBI, FBI, FBI.

To Summarise

In this chapter you've discovered some of the finishing touches you can add to your mix...the importance of rapport, how open questions give you the nuggets of information you need to instigate your service or offer, how to use IPA to make sure you're doing enough to create new sales opportunities and how FBI can help you prioritise your activity.

What are your three priority actions that you're going to take as a result of reading this chapter?

1 ....

2 ....

3 ....

Go do them as quickly as you can

...anytime **NOW** would be good.

How are you doing with your action points from each chapter?

As you've now worked through the book, you will have at least 27 actions listed. Take a look back now and count how many of these you have completed; how many you have partially completed; and how many you have yet to start.

Celebrate the actions you've taken. Congratulations!!! How have they worked for you? What can you do to make the results even better? How have these actions changed you as a person?

Then there are the actions you haven't taken. What stops you? What would you like instead? What's your positive intention for not doing them? Explore this for yourself and if you still procrastinate get help from someone that you know who will hold you to account and support you to get them done.

If you've taken on even half the things you've learned in this book you will now be experiencing better relationships, a stronger pipeline and more success generating sales. It doesn't stop with that. If you read this book again you'll be reading it from a different starting point with different perspectives and beliefs...and guess what...you'll get a whole bunch of different actions because you are in a different place.

So I urge you to re-read this book and keep taking new actions to develop yourself to be the best you can be.

This is your journey to greater success so be sure to enjoy it.

It's been a pleasure sharing it with you

10

If you Manage a Sales Team

"The task of the leader is to get their people from where they are to where they have not been."

— Henry Kissinger

Being a sales leader

If you manage a sales team you will definitely know the highs when your team are a well oiled machine in flow and the lows when they are out of sync...or anywhere in between.

Being a sales leader can be a thankless task and one that needs a wide and diverse range of skills that really keep you on your toes. At any given moment you switch between being a mentor, coach, counsellor, analyst, social worker, leader, motivator...you name it...you're it!

You know that your team need to be in the best possible state to deliver high levels of sales so you do what you have to do to keep them there.

Reading this book will have gone some way to giving you an insight into the patterns that people have...clients, prospects...and of courses your sales team!

This part of the book is designed to help you take everything you've read in terms of generating sales and use it to have greater understanding and more tools to inspire and motivate your team.

You may well have already come up with some pointers of your own but knowing how the mind works, my guess is that you'll have been focusing on how to close more sales with a view to passing the techniques on to your team.

It's now time to focus on how you can develop an outstanding team.

Ready?

You train your team how to treat you

The way you interact with each member of your team will cause them to behave in a particular way. They will do certain things and not do others.

If they do something that you are unhappy with and you say nothing, unconsciously you are saying that it's OK for them to continue. If members of your team are not doing specific activities you really want them to and you ignore it, you're saying it's OK not to do it. You may not be using words, you'll be using actions and you know that actions speak louder than words.

You absolutely must communicate what you want and what you don't want. Your team are not mind readers so don't expect them to be.

Your team need to know the rules, the boundaries and what's expected in order to deliver what you want...and when they get it wrong you need to communicate how they got it wrong and discuss the way forward...even the little things.

If you're not completely confident in this approach I have one thing to say...GET CONFIDENT. You will never lead a winning team unless you master this basic principle. Do whatever you need to do to get you there. This is critical. There are lots of techniques in this book to help you. You will be doing yourself and your team a massive service...and you'll generate more sales.

Imagine a team that knows exactly what's expected of them...what's acceptable...what's not...and getting the job done. Imagine the kudos for you!!! Worth it? You bet.

Stop Telling

What do you do when one of your team come to you for advice? It is so important that you're able to distinguish between when to give advice and when not.

Imagine for a moment that one of your sales team come to you because they're not sure how to do something. How do you handle the situation?

I've worked with so many sales managers and directors that fall into the trap of thinking that telling someone how to do something is the same as teaching them how to do it. If you've noticed specific sales people making the same mistake time and time again, my guess is that you could be continually telling them what to do and they're just not doing it. Frustrating isn't it?

Whenever you tell your team the best way to do stuff (and I know you're doing this with the best positive intention) you train them not to think for themselves. You create an environment where they feel the need to run stuff by you to confirm it's right.

The very best way to develop your team is to ask them what they think they should do. This develops their mind to come up with their own solutions. My approach is "I have some thoughts but what do you think?" Most of the time they come up with a perfectly good solution and I can reinforce their thinking by congratulating them and supporting them to get started. If their solution gets the job done (even if mine is simpler, faster, easier) I let them get on with it. This is the only way they have complete ownership. They will learn from the process. Let them scuff their knees...it's a great way to learn.

If their solution is way off track, ask lots of questions that give them their own realisation of the potential consequences of their solution. "What would happen if...." Help them develop a new solution for themselves.

This not only develops your team to think for themselves, it empowers them, grows confidence, increases contribution and self worth and creates new pathways in their thinking.

You have enough to do without having to think for them too! Remember...you train your team how to treat you. What are you training them to do if you keep giving them the answers?

Put them back at 'Cause'

When you notice one of your team coming up with reasons or excuses for not achieving, your role as their leader is to take them out of 'effect' and put them at 'cause'.

When one of your team is in 'effect' they have the potential to impact on every other member. Think about it...one of them says 'all my clients have frozen their budgets'...or 'the economy is poor and nobody is spending'. Another person that may be struggling a little decides that's the reason they're not doing well. People jump on any bandwagon that makes sense to them, especially if it blames something or someone else for their own lack of sales. It's very common...and very human.

When your team are in 'effect' they become victims and will be less likely to give 100% to any sales activity. It's just too difficult or not worth the effort. Your job will be like pushing your team uphill whilst they sleep...bloody challenging!

A great question when your team use reasons or excuses is..."OK if all that is true, what action are you going to take to ensure you achieve your target?"

This question puts them straight back at 'cause' and allows their unconscious mind to come up with solutions. Make sure that they come up with as many solutions as possible by asking "What else could you do?" Evaluate every solution they come up with and help them decide on specific actions to keep them on track.

Develop your ability to notice these reasons and excuses and deal with them immediately they are uttered so you can nip it in the bud.

Feedback

Get comfortable with giving all feedback...and do it at the earliest opportunity.

It's really easy to give positive feedback and great to do it when plenty of others can hear. It positively reinforces the individual getting the feedback and creates a desire in the others to be on the receiving end of it in the future. It reinforces good behaviour!!

When you give feedback that's more negative in nature this absolutely must be done in a one to one setting. Rapport is vital and it must come from a positive perspective. This is all about learning from things that didn't go as planned. There's no such thing as failure. There are only results...some you like and some you don't. It's from the results you don't like where the biggest learning's are. What can you both learn from what happened? Yes there will be learning for you too. How did you contribute to this result? You are not blameless. It may be something that you did..or something that you didn't do. What would have got a different result?

Get them to suggest action points that move them towards a positive outcome. This will create a much higher motivation to complete the actions and achieve the agreed objective.

Communication is the response it elicits!

It's not what you think you said...it's what the other person thinks you said that's important.

Whenever I ask a member of my team for something and I get something else, I ask myself...what did I say that made them decide this was what I wanted?

It is your responsibility to ensure 100% understanding of what you have said...and the way you ask is crucial.

Can you please feed that back to me so that I can be sure I've given you everything you need?

If you ask "Can you feed that back to me so that I can be sure you've understood?" places the responsibility for the communication squarely on them. That's abdicating in my book. Take responsibility by giving yourself time to craft your messages and you'll have a team with greater understanding who are more united in the cause to be the best.

Match preferences

Most people communicate with the outside world in a way that works for them. As a sales leader it's crucially important that you communicate with each individual using their own preferences...Representational Systems and Meta Programmes.

If you have someone in your team that has a strong visual preference be sure to follow up conversations with an email. If they are auditory, have a conversation...do not just send an email. If you have a kinaesthetic person on your team focus on their feelings and for the auditory digital, it's all about logic and making sense.

Probably the most important Meta Programme for you to focus on is the motivation filter of Towards and Away From.

Whatever your preference you absolutely must match 'Towards' and 'Away From' psychology. Your 'Towards' people will be motivated by incentives, prizes, money, acknowledgement...in fact any reward normally works!

If you have 'Away From' people in your team you will need to associate them into the pain or consequences of not achieving. The stronger the potential pain...the more motivated they will be.

Get it the wrong way round and you'll have a bunch of demotivated people around you...and demotivated sales people don't generate many sales!!!

When you're addressing the team as a whole you'll need to incorporate all preferences in your approach.

Check out the following for as many preferences as you can:

Some of you will be really excited about next year and the incentives to play for and some of you may be worried that you're not able to achieve these targets. Whatever you're thinking, that's fine because as a team you have all the skills to show this company how great you can be...and I will support you in every way that I can. Decide for yourself what's important to you to make this happen. You may need a logical systematic approach...or you may want to focus on images of success...some of you may want regular discussions to keep you on track and some of you may want to imagine how you'll feel when you've achieved success.

How many preferences did you spot?

Develop your ability to use specific ones with individuals and all of them when your team are together.

Good language

The words you use when communicating will impact on the internal state of your team.

Using positive language will make yours and their lives much easier.

For example, many years ago I had a personal fitness trainer who when showing me a new exercise used to say...this is really hard but I know that you can do it Leigh. It was his way of giving me a compliment.

If you do this with your team you are creating an expectation that it will be hard. It's much better to say...this may not be easy at first but it will get easier each time you use it.

You must focus their attention on empowering words and states. Remember the brain will give you more of what you focus on. When you hear the people in your team use negative or disempowering language your mission is to acknowledge where they are then reframe it for them.

> They say:
>
> *I'm having a really tough day...can't get anyone on the phone...everyone's on voicemail.*
>
> You say:
>
> *OK...so you're not having the easiest day today but it's a great opportunity to work on your voicemail message to test which one works best in getting a response.*

Mastering reframing will keep your team productive and positive and make managing them a dream.

An important word that you can use to good effect is *BUT*. It deletes what precedes it so use it wisely.

OK so you didn't win this one **but** *you have a great pipeline*

Is much better than...

You have a great pipeline **but** *you didn't win this one.*

People will always focus on what comes after the BUT so make sure it's the positive stuff!!

It's also worth noting that if in conversation with one of your team around performance and they say 'Yes but....' it means they don't agree with you at all and you need to do a better job of communicating your message!

Oh yes... *however* is a *but* in a tuxedo ☺

The top sales leadership tips

I'm going to give you some pointers based on the topics covered in each chapter that you can use with your team to inspire, motivate and boost your sales.

1. How your thinking determines your sales success

Understand that every member of your sales team is unique. They have different maps of the world that cause them to focus in different ways. They will process and store information in their own way. Your role is to understand their map of the world and communicate with them in a way that's right for them...irrespective of your own preferences. This isn't about agreeing with their map...it's about acknowledging it and honouring where they are.

If you want to influence your team, it's crucial that you are able to identify each person's preferences, their values and beliefs. You will need to be really flexible in your approach in order to take them from where they are to where they need to be to achieve success and contribute to the team.

Pointers to focus on:

- Acknowledge where they are, identify the gap, decide what would best bridge that gap to suit their preferences
- Use language that creates a positive internal state
- Say what you want clearly so nobody has to guess. Remember that people will interpret your words differently
- Communicate the objectives to focus their attention on the right things
- Separate their behaviours from the language used. It doesn't matter how many times they say they will do it if they're not actually doing it
- Reinforce their skills by acknowledging good performance
- Listen out for reasons and excuses and ask "What action can you take to get you closer to your desired outcome?" Put them back at 'cause'
- Deal with poor performance or their personal state immediately
- Remember...you train people how to treat you!!!
- Feedback...feedback...feedback

Based on these pointers...what are your three priority actions that would have the biggest impact on increasing the sales success of your team?

1 ....

2 ....

3 ....

2. How your beliefs impact your thinking...and your results

What your team believe will have a huge impact on how your team performs.

Unless you've had therapy training you may not be able to get rid of deep rooted limiting beliefs but the Belief Buster will really help you to move people when they are stuck and in most cases can be all that's needed to make huge shifts in a person's thinking.

Your role is to help individuals in your team to consciously identify the limiting beliefs that get in the way of their sales success. As most limiting beliefs are unconscious it really is up to you to dig them out.

Pointers to focus on:

- Notice the activities that individuals avoid and follow it up with "What stops you?" Always have these conversations in private as they can sometimes become emotional
- Listen to the language that your team use. Limited beliefs are often unconsciously stated without the person even realising

- Guide individuals in your team through the Belief Buster a couple of times to check understanding of the process. They can then do it on their own as often as they need afterwards

Based on these pointers...what are your three priority actions that would have the biggest impact on increasing the sales success of your team?

1 ....

2 ....

3 ....

3. Sales and the inner you

We all have inner dialogue...both positive and negative. It's when the balance is tipped predominantly towards the negative that your leadership role becomes challenging.

Working with your team to eliminate their limiting beliefs will go a long way to reducing negative internal dialogue.

You can also notice changes in physiology when a person is experiencing their inner critic. You'll see things like rolling of eyes, screwing up of faces and the like – calibrate what's normal for each member of your team and look out for differences.

Pointers to focus on:

- Use positive language at all times to reinforce a positive internal dialogue
- Notice resistance to certain tasks
- Ask them "What are you thinking?"

- Negative internal dialogue often stems from limiting beliefs and is a clue that something deeper is going on
- Use 'chunking up' to gain agreement and clarity
- Use 'Parts Integration' when you find inner conflict

Based on these pointers...what are your three priority actions that would have the biggest impact on increasing the sales success of your team?

1 ....

2 ....

3 ....

4. Putting yourself in the right state of mind

When members of your team are not in the best state of mind your role is to shift and lift their state. It's only when sales people are in a good state that you maximise the potential level of sales.

Their inner state is influenced by so much...both in and out of work...and you will need to use different tactics with each person to identify the triggers.

Pointers to focus on:

- Calibrate each member of your team – what works for each of them to lift their state
- Make the environment in which they work as positive as possible
- Give positive feedback for good performance

- Give improvement feedback in a positive way
- Introduce friendly competition and FUN
- Get together as much as possible
- Point out the consequences of maintaining a less than positive state (this will work especially well for individuals with an 'Away From' preference)
- Create anchors to positive events
- Introduce the 'Circle of Excellence'

Based on these pointers...what are your three priority actions that would have the biggest impact on increasing the sales success of your team?

1 ....

2 ....

3 ....

5. Managing your inner software to achieve more sales

Once you have identified the individual preferences of your team your job will become so much easier.

You'll understand why they do the things they do in the way that they do it, how to motivate and inspire them, how to give feedback that influences their thinking...and how to get them to generate more sales.

It's the fairy dust!

Pointers to focus on:

- Calibrate each and every one of them...Representational System and Meta Programme preferences
- Develop a strategy for each person in your team for 1 to 1 sessions, appraisals, on the job coaching, best communication method...in fact every single interaction you have with them
- Be on the lookout for every clue to their personal preferences...right down to the best time of day to interact with them dependant on your outcome
- Construct your communication specifically for each individual. One size definitely does not fit all
- Use all preferences when you get together as a team for maximum impact, influence and to generate a real team spirit

Based on these pointers...what are your three priority actions that would have the biggest impact on increasing the sales success of your team?

1 ....

2 ....

3 ....

6. The next step

This is all about outcomes. It's so important that you know what each of your team really want to achieve...and if they don't know you need to help them identify what that outcome is.

They already know that they have to achieve sales...that's a given. Chunking up to why that's important will really give you leverage to inspire and motivate.

The models in this chapter not only give your team a framework to follow...they also increase the commitment and motivation to achieve...even when procrastination rears its ugly head!

Pointers to focus on:

Always focus on outcomes...yours and your team

Monitor the actions they plan and keep them on track

Hold them accountable for their results

Point out any clues that procrastination may be setting in. People are often in denial when this starts to happen

Based on these pointers...what are your three priority actions that would have the biggest impact on increasing the sales success of your team?

1 ....

2 ....

3 ....

7. Modelling sales success

This is an absolute must for you to incorporate. If you can elicit the strategy of the most successful member of your team...you can replicate it in the others. As if by magic!

You will have already calibrated what is poor, good or great performance. You need to go beyond what you see and elicit the inner workings of the individual to really understand their strategy.

Once you've understood this...the world is your oyster!

Pointers to focus on:

- Seek out high achievers...in and outside your organisation
- Use the process in this book to elicit as much as you can about their strategy
- Remember that a successful strategy needs to be a good fit if someone is to take it on consistently. Have a number of strategies for each element of sales success
- If you notice resistance in taking on another strategy explore where it doesn't work for them. Sometimes leaving out a small element makes it a better match and could still achieve the same result
- Be very clear about what exactly you want to model. Break it down into individual skills

Based on these pointers...what are your three priority actions that would have the biggest impact on increasing the sales success of your team?

1 ....

2 ....

3 ....

8. Measuring up

In order to know that you are going in the right direction you need to assess your KPI's...you'll know this already.

What you need to start measuring is what goes on in the heads of your team to boost your results.

Start to measure activities that measure their thinking processes and remember to give feedback on all aspects of their performance.

Pointers to focus on:

- Have a monthly one to one session with each person to assess how they are doing against their objectives...both physical and mental KPI's
- Congratulate them when they are on track
- Support them through the challenging times. DO NOT tell them how to get through this...they need to work it out for themselves
- Help them find a mentor that they respect and can learn from...this will be in addition to the relationship they already have with you

- Use the Quantum Questions to give clarity
- Use *The 5 Keys to Sales Success* to keep you on track

Based on these pointers...what are your three priority actions that would have the biggest impact on increasing the sales success of your team?

1 ....

2 ....

3 ....

9. Putting it all Together

Rapport...rapport...rapport!

When you have great levels of rapport with your team they will do anything for you. This doesn't mean being their best buddy...far from it.

You're their boss and there needs to be boundaries. You need to communicate when they're good and you need to communicate even more effectively when they're not! Whatever the situation you can definitely have great rapport and respect.

Without rapport you're unlikely to get the results you want on a consistent basis.

Pointers to focus on:

- Getting into their map of the world is the best way to establish and maintain rapport
- Use their preferences in your communication to influence their thinking and move them constantly towards their full potential

- Extract solutions from them to get buy in...especially around IPA and FBI
- Use open questions to establish what's going on for them. Avoid 'why' questions which could seriously jeopardise your levels of rapport
- Respect their map of the world even if you don't agree with it and work with them to find a way of getting from point A to point B
- Leave your judgement at home

...and most importantly...

- Get your team to read this book ☺

Based on these pointers...what are your three priority actions that would have the biggest impact on increasing the sales success of your team?

1 ....

2 ....

3 ....

Now I know you want to be the very best leader that you can be...with the most successful team on record.

You want to be remembered for all the right reasons and none of the wrong ones.

Whatever your motivation for reading this book,
I congratulate you.

Not only have you discovered my thoughts on how to generate sales...you also know my thoughts on leading and developing an outstanding team.

The strategies in this book work. I've tested them all and so have my clients.

Now it's your turn to test them for yourself.

It's been an honour to share this part of your journey with you.

To your continued success, happiness and of course
enormous sales!

The end...which really, is only the beginning! ☺

Case Studies and Testimonials

Euro London

Psychology in Sales and Communication training programme ran from March 2009 to May 2010

The reason Leigh was called in was that we needed something different to add value to our sales force.

Whilst they had been trained by usual sales trainers they were still not always putting into practice the training they had and sales were not increasing.

What Leigh brought to the table was the ability to give our staff confidence and to adapt themselves to the client etc...

Sales Results

Initially, 2009 Qtr 2 Revenues (i.e. those revenues resulting from mainly Qtr 1 sales activity) fell 39% v 2009 Qtr 1 – reiterating the need for the programme.

- The programme commenced March 2009
- From 2009 Qtr 3 to 2010 Qtr 4, ***5 out of 6 Qtrs registered an increase over the previous Qtr***
- The total increase in Quarterly revenues from 2009 Qtr 3 to 2010 Qtr 4 was **+67%**
- ***Sales per head also rose 67% during the same period*** (Headcount had remained static)
- ***This performance was achieved against an industry drop of 12%*** during the same period

— Steve Shacklock, Managing Director, Euro London

Blackbook

Leigh Ashton has delivered training programmes since August 2007.

Initially, we had a situation where, apart from the occasional month, sales revenues had been falling consistently versus the same periods a year earlier. We had 25 in the sales team and on the whole, motivation levels were falling too.

We had a vicious circle of low confidence and low motivation resulting in decreasing sales and so on.

I met Leigh Ashton after a recommendation from an HR consultant. I was struck by Leigh's enthusiasm from the first meeting and after experiencing her taster session we designed a programme together which fitted the needs of the team. Crucially the team were enthused too. They didn't want or need 'run of the mill' sales training and this clearly was not that!

It was clear from session one that Leigh was having an impact. Attitudes seemingly changed overnight and with it motivation levels.

As the sessions progressed Leigh instilled new levels of drive in the team and I was very impressed by how they became much more responsible for their own performance. Enthusiasm levels rose and even relationships with other colleagues improved.

The acid test (were sales increasing) was soon passed. We were soon having more productive client meetings which fed through to conversions and extra sales on the board. Checking back, from the third month of the programme (when Leigh's impact was becoming embedded within the team) monthly sales averaged 27% more than the corresponding month from a year earlier.

This average increase has been sustained since the programme finished and we plan to have Leigh back for refresher training on an ongoing basis.

I would be delighted to recommend Leigh as a training professional who can positively change attitudes, motivation levels, personal beliefs around selling, confidence – and the sales figures!

— Paul Cushing, Managing Director, BlackBook

Harrods

"Incredibly useful. Learned new techniques and methods that will really help me in my role."

— Charlotte Marks, Sales Director, Harrods

Diamond Build Plc

"The team all did remarkably well and worked their socks off.... pure sales. Your techniques kicked in and they had a completely different approach to previous events. Thanks!"

— Steve Boniface, Managing Director, Diamond Build

Amber Raney-Kincade

"I am still using her amazing techniques.... 2 months after the seminar!"

— Amber Raney-Kincade, Marketing Consultant

Cathay Pacific

"Excellent session with immediate practical applications. Leigh is clear, confident, passionate and used lots of examples."

— Paul Cruttenden, Sales Director, Cathay Pacific

ITV

"Educational, Motivational, Inspiring. Positive, articulate with good explanations."

— Stephen Poole, Online Sales, ITV

You may also like to check Leigh's recommendations on Linked In. You'll find them here:

http://www.linkedin.com/pub/leigh-ashton/0/99/424

Notes

Whatever your sales challenge ...there is a solution!

Contact me:

Tel: 020 7903 5426

email: leigh@sales-consultancy.com

Find out more:

www.sales-consultancy.com

Follow me:

http://twitter.com/#!/nlpSalesSuccess

https://www.facebook.com/SalesConsultancy

Be inspired to take action!

Sell

About the author

Leigh Ashton is an author, speaker, trainer and coach. She helps sales professionals and business owners get more sales. Companies turn to her when they've tried everything to increase sales productivity... and they're still not getting the results they want.

Leigh has been in sales since 1984 and many moons ago as a young sales manager she became frustrated with the inconsistent performance of her sales team.

This motivated her to go and find out why this happens...and crucially how to fix it. She discovered that what goes on inside a person's head has the biggest impact on whether they achieve sales success or not.

Since 1986 Leigh has trained thousands of people to use psychology to make positive changes to their attitude, their approach and their sales results.

Leigh's approach takes people through a process that:

- Helps them identify their psychological barriers and gives them the tools to overcome them
- Teaches them how the mind works so they can keep motivated and stay focussed
- Gives them the ability to identify the psychological patterns of their clients and prospects so they connect with them at a deeper level and close more sales

And at a higher level...

- It creates more success in other areas of their lives so they are happier generally...and happier people generate more sales

She is known for inspiring sales professionals and business owners to take action and increase sales anywhere from 20 to over 100%.

Her approach is aimed at the psychology that influences people's sales results. The techniques she uses identify and resolve these inner issues at source. Changes become embedded at a deeper level and therefore the new behaviour is sustainable and long term.

Leigh says..."So many people struggle with selling. I absolutely know that I can help them identify their barriers to success...I know I can give them the tools to eliminate what's holding them back...and ultimately...I can enable them to achieve massive sales success".

Lightning Source UK Ltd.
Milton Keynes UK
UKOW030212120412

190553UK00001B/2/P

9 781907 722660